The Miracles of Mentoring

The Miracles of Mentoring

HOW TO ENCOURAGE AND LEAD FUTURE GENERATIONS

Thomas W. Dortch, Jr.
and The 100 Black Men of America, Inc.

BROADWAY BOOKS
New York

A hardcover edition of this book was originally published in 2000 by Doubleday, a division of Random House, Inc.

Designed by Richard Oriolo

The Library of Congress has cataloged the hardcover as:

Dortch, Thomas W.
The miracles of mentoring: how to encourage and lead future generations / Thomas W. Dortch, Jr.
p. cm.
1. Children and adults. 2. Mentoring. 3. Afro-American children—Psychology.
4. Afro-American teenagers—Psychology. I. Title.
BF723.P25.D67 2000
158'.3—dc21 99-089128

ISBN 0-7679-0574-1

This book is dedicated to my family: my mother, Lizzie Dortch; my late father, Thomas W. Dortch, Sr.; my sisters, Carolyn, Marie, and Juanita; my brother Richard and my late brother John; my wife, Carole; and my children, Thomas III, Angelique, Mark, Bridgette, and Mulu.

Thank you for your love, prayers, honesty, coaching, sacrifice, and hope for my success.

Thanks for being there during the good times and the times of challenge. You have been the fuel of my fire of desire.

Acknowledgments

I was fortunate to have a wonderful childhood because of caring adults who were concerned about the safety, security, and development of the youth in my community. I thank: Willie Mae Keels, Betty Henderson, Adeline Canady, Billy Latin, Francis Martin, Professor Thomas, Mrs. Woodruff, Mrs. Wilson, Robert Holly, Clarence Wilson, James Neal, Robert Strubble, G. J. Lee, Booth Ramsey, and C. A. Scott.

Education is the key to success and success is a journey not a destination. I thank those who helped me along my path: Wilson Gosier, Thomas J. Palmer, Samuel Jolly, Ozias Pearson, Barbara Palmer, Elaine Baker, the late Dr. W. W. E. Blanchet, the late Dr. C. W. Pettigrew, the late Dr. Pierro, J. D. Smith, Dr. Kofi Bota, and Dr. Luther Burse.

I have been blessed to have so many friends, mentors, and positive images in my life who have served as beacon lights to guide me whether on smooth or bumpy roads. These individuals have helped me to remain focused and have encouraged me to seek excellence without excuse: Sam Nunn, John Lewis, Andrew Young, Julian Bond, Lonnie King, the late Jondelle Johnson, Jessie Hill, Charlie Graves, the late Ben Brown, Maynard Jackson, Hank Aaron, Dr. Julian Earls, Earl Graves, Thomas N. Todd, Walt

Bellamy, Dr. James Kaufmann, the late Marjorie Thurman, Lottie Watkins, Therman McKenzie, Claybon Edwards, the late Carrie Mays, Xernona Clayton, Bob Goodwin, Al Gore, Kweisi Mfume, Herman Russell, Bill Campbell, Governor George Busbee, George Fraser, Dennis Archer, Nathaniel Goldston, James "Mac" Hunter, Elridge McMillan, Sal Diaz-Verson, Benjamin Barksdale, Connie Carr, Wayman Smith, Lewis McKinney, Dennis Malamatinas, Dr. Harold Wade, Dr. Ben Hooks, Lenny Springs, Evern Cooper, Ed Bowen, Dr. Bobby Austin, Curley Dossman, Clem Childs, Clarence Smith, Coretta Scott King, Dr. C. T. Vivian, Dr. Billy Black, Tom Cordy, Herman Reese, Ingrid Saunders Jones, the late Dr. Nelson McGhee, Dr. Joe Johnson, Rev. Joe Roberts, Rev. Joseph Lowery, Calvin Smyre, Al Dotson, Sr., Jim Thompson, Moses Brewer, Miranda Mack McKenzie, Esther Silver Parker, Elizabeth Waters, Ron Williams, Rudolph Terry, Willie Gregory, Eugene McCullers, Dr. Thomas Cole, Jr., Larry Wallace, Dr. Johnetta Cole, Gene Parker, the late Bill Giles, Dr. Jim Black, Geri Thomas, Tony Grant, Deborah Poole, Dr. Hilliard Lackey, Donald Wade, the late William Wimberly, and Dr. Robert Wright.

To the very special team that helped to make this book a reality, thank you for your support, guidance, and inspiration: Janet Hill, Carla Fine, Barbara Lowenstein, Madeleine Morel, Alexander Kopelman, Dr. Joshua Murfree, Thomas W. Dortch III, George Fraser, Dwayne Ashley, Donna Carter Butler, Jan Joell, Brenda Cantrell, Eunice Lockhart Moss, Shelley Nelson, Paula Collins, the Men of the "100," the Mentees, and their parents.

Contents

Foreword

In 1999, I was named Man of the Year by the 100 Black Men of America, Inc. Now granted, my fantasy was to be named Man of the Year by 100 Black Women . . . but I was very honored, just the same. I've always been impressed with the organization and have much respect for its Miracles of Mentoring program. So, when my fraternity brother Thomas Dortch asked me to write the Foreword to his book, *The Miracles of Mentoring,* I didn't hesitate. I'm excited about any book that helps people become better mentors to young children.

Tommy's experience of being "reared" by the whole community in his hometown of Toccoa, Georgia, immediately reminded me of my upbringing. I can honestly say that as a child growing up in Tuskeegee, Alabama, I was surrounded by positive role models who had a direct influence in shaping my life. As I got older, I realized that every child isn't as lucky as I was. There are many kids out there who have no positive model to look up to, and that's why organizations like 100 Black Men are so crucial. You've read the statistics, you've watched the news, you've seen Master P's videos—it's no secret that young black people, young black males in particular, are faced with some horrible choices as they strive to reach adulthood in our society.

It's easy to tell them to say no to drugs and gang activity, but the hard part is showing them an alternative that they can find acceptable. It takes skill, dedication, commitment, and patience, not to mention the ability to use slang words in the right context.

For 30 years, 100 Black Men has stepped up to the plate and, through its mentoring programs, it has given our youth the kinds of alternatives they need to help keep them on the right track. And now, 100 Black Men is sharing its successful mentoring program with the world.

How many times have you asked, "I'd like to help a child, but I don't know what to do"? Or said, "I don't have the time. I don't have anything to offer. I can't afford it." I promise you, by the time you finish reading this book, all of these questions will be answered.

If you know anything about me, or the *Tom Joyner Morning Show*, you know our goal is to move people to action, and that's exactly what this book does. It isn't enough to just sit around and talk about what's wrong with our society. Like 100 Black Men, the *Tom Joyner Morning Show* tries to make a difference by getting people to become proactive. Every morning on our syndicated radio program we reach millions of African Americans, and aside from entertaining them with music and a few laughs we also try to give them the tools to transform them from listeners to activists.

For years, local black radio has played a central role in the lives of black people. We depend on local radio to speak to us directly about our communities. Even though our radio program is national and can be heard on nearly 100 syndicated stations across the country, our listeners still tune in each morning and depend on us to tell them what they need to know, and more important, what they need to be doing. When we do our job right, our audience feels better about themselves and their communities. That's because they're able to see the results of their actions: to record voter turn out; to see thousands of dollars raised to help black kids go to college through the Tom Joyner Foundation; to implement changes in national policy; even to witness a Congressional Gold Medal for Rosa Parks, the "mother" of the Civil Rights movement. We can't always take credit for the fire, but we can take credit for the spark, and sometimes a little spark is all it takes.

100 Black Men has been very successful at shedding light on the lives of young black people by identifying their need for positive black male role models, and by filling that need. Times are changing. It's no longer realistic to assume that every kid has a dad, an uncle, or a big brother to call on for advice, help with homework, or just get a pat on the back. So the question is: Are we going to sit back and talk about the problem, or are we going to be pro-active and do something about it?

I've talked a lot about how mentoring programs help young people, but it's a two-way street. Talk to anybody who has served as a mentor and he or she will tell you how rewarding it is. It's especially rewarding for black men like those in the 100 who get a chance to give something back, and to be appreciated in a society that isn't always that appreciative.

I applaud the 100 Black Men of America, Inc., for providing black males an opportunity to shine in the eyes of their kids, their communities, and their nation. And I applaud them even more for sharing their winning formula in this book. Read it and go out and make a difference in the life of a child.

—TOM JOYNER

The Miracles of Mentoring

INTRODUCTION

The More You Give, the More You Get: Choosing to Make a Difference

A tree cannot stand without its roots.

—AFRICAN PROVERB

In 1988, as I lay in the hospital facing a rare form of cancer, I did not know whether I would live long enough to see my two-year-old boy and ten-year-old girl grow up. Through surgery, chemotherapy, and faith, the struggle to reclaim my life from the shadow of death, I had to deal with feelings of fear, anguish, and uncertainty. The one thing I did not feel, however, was regret. In confronting mortality, I realized that I was proud of the choices I had made in my life.

Since my college days, I worked hard to strengthen community and country. I always wanted my children to have a better world to live in, whether I were in it or not. I always wanted to leave a legacy.

We all want to live on in some way after we have gone—in words, deeds, monuments, memories. We want a part of ourselves to be woven into the fabric of the world. My way of doing this has always been to give the best parts of myself to the people around me by serving as a role model, a guide, a trusted friend—a mentor. That was what I had learned growing up: that we all stand on the shoulders of the people who came before us and that it is our duty to support those who come after.

Now, as I battled illness, I found great solace in the knowledge that I had succeeded in living up to a standard that my elders would be proud of. And the outpouring of love and goodwill from the people I had helped along the way—especially the young people whose lives I had touched as a mentor—gave me the strength and determination to go on. As I got better, I focused my energies on the things that were now more important than ever: family, community, and young people.

Since I became the president of the 100 Black Men of America, Inc., in 1994, I have worked to expand and diversify the organization's mentoring programs. This book is part of our efforts to inspire and shape the lives of our children, bring hope and opportunity to poor and neglected neighborhoods, and put jails out of business once and for all.

Our hope is that this book will help readers experience

the satisfaction of seeing a young person they have mentored blossom into a strong, independent human being. Our goal is to help as many young people as possible to benefit from having someone to look up to, someone who cares about their future, someone who believes in them.

Back to the Barbershop

When I was a boy, growing up in Toccoa, Georgia, we had the whole community looking out for our children. There were James Neal, the town mortician who later became the mayor, and Mr. Clarence Wilson, the electrician. There were Miss Canady and Miss Henderson and Miss Keels over at the school. And of course there were Mr. Scott and Mr. Holley, the barbers. You could not get into trouble anywhere in our small North Georgia town without an adult there to set you straight or to take care of you if you were hurt or hurting. As children, we relied on the knowledge that there were all these adults who loved us and looked out for us.

For us boys, it was the regular trip to the barbershop that gave us a cut on life. We would get our trims and then hang around, enjoying the company of older men who gathered there to play checkers and dominoes and exchange news and stories. We would listen to the elders toss around expressions like "Every dog knows his bone" and "If you make your bed, you've got to sleep in it" and know that we were picking up bits of their wisdom.

Occasionally, one of the men would call you over and ask how you were doing in school and whether you were staying out of trouble. Questions such as "What are you going to do with your life?" were common, and they demanded real answers. On those Saturday mornings, we learned to respect our elders and to value community.

None of us knew it at the time, but the barbershop was one of the special places where we went to be mentored. All of us anticipated and enjoyed the moments when one of the older men would look up from his newspaper or his game of checkers and say: "You're Tom's boy, right? Well, what have you got to say for yourself?" This was not idle conversation; these men really wanted to know that we were on the right track. And it made us feel important to have so many adults investing their hopes in our future.

These are different times, though, and barbershops have been largely replaced by impersonal buzz-cut mills and chain salons. Close-knit communities like the Toccoa of my boyhood days are fast disappearing, as the fabric and focus of our society continues to change. Most children have few opportunities for the kind of casual give-and-take with adults who helped me and my friends grow up. This is particularly distressing in light of the fact that families, to a large extent, can no longer provide children with the full range of the durable adult relationships crucial to their development.

Just consider these numbers for a second: Only 40 percent of all the young people in this country can expect to spend their entire childhood living with both biological parents. Nearly 15 million children live in single parent homes. And almost two and a half million children under the age of 13 are unsupervised after school lets out for the day.

"It takes a village to raise a child," the African proverb wisely states. And now, more than ever, we need the whole "village" to pitch in to give our kids the care and nurturing they need. We cannot leave it up to schools and youth-serving organizations to do the whole job. We must create virtual communities to provide children with the guidance, support, and role models necessary to help them explore their worlds, dream their dreams, and work toward making those dreams into reality. These goals can be accomplished if each of us steps up and accepts the responsibilities, the joys, and the miracles of mentoring.

What Is a Mentor?

If you look up the word *mentor* in the dictionary, you will find that it means a "trusted guide," a "provider of wise counsel," a "confidant." Throughout history, mentors have emerged as advice givers. Long before formal schooling or workplace training came into existence, these individuals served as a major source of knowledge. They accepted the responsibilities and challenges of preparing their protégés by sharing with them the expertise and practical know-how gained through their own experiences.

Approximately 14 million youths under the age of 18 in the United States—half of the entire youth population in this country—are defined as "at risk" of getting into trouble; 7 million of them—or a quarter of all young people—are considered "very high risk." These statistics are sobering reminders that we as a society are failing our children in some fundamental ways.

Mentoring is a way to make a dent in these numbers by providing guidance and fostering support and encouragement for these vulnerable young people. Mentoring is open to everyone, and people from all walks of life participate in hundreds of diverse and interesting mentoring programs throughout the country. By becoming a mentor, you will touch the life of a child, make a difference for tomorrow's youth, and give back to your community by investing in a young person who will, in turn, mentor the next generation.

Mentors come in all shapes and sizes. If you close your eyes and think about all the people who have influenced your life, you will come up with your own personal definition of the word. Some mentors played a central role in decisions you made and paths you chose; others touched you even without your awareness, yet had a profound effect on your very being.

When people ask me what it takes to be a mentor, I always think back to Billy Latin, a handyman who worked for my father, and the lesson he taught me about life. I had just turned sixteen and had been driving with my learner's permit for almost a year. My dad said, "Tommy, you need to get your permit renewed. Now that you're sixteen, you can try later this year to pass the test to get a driver's license." And he asked Billy to take me down to the State Trooper Station.

On the way over, Billy said, "Boy, why don't you go straight for your driver's license. No big boy like you needs to be driving around with just a permit. And if you don't go in there and pass that test, you're going to have to walk all the way back home."

So I went and took the test and knocked it out. I took the driver's exam with the state trooper, and passed without a hitch. Billy let me drive back home and I saw him looking at me from the passenger seat. "Now that you got your driver's license," he grinned, "tell your dad that you need a car!"

Here was Billy, a man who made a living sweeping up

other people's yards and doing odd jobs, caring enough about me—and believing in me—to insist that I live up to my full potential. That is a lesson I have never forgotten. And it is at the heart of what mentoring means to me: caring adults helping young people to see the options available to them, allowing them to define themselves, and then making it safe for them to become the people they want to be.

We must not accept the erroneous belief, however, that only youths whose lives are affected by poverty, drugs, and violence need our support and guidance. As Dwayne Ashley, the former executive director of the 100 Black Men of America, reminds us, childhood and adolescence are periods of rapid change and adaptation, during which all children need a lot of support: "Growing up is a scary time. There are so many changes, so much confusion. A mentor is someone who helps to take some of the fear out of a kid's life."

Mentors are not social workers or surrogate parents or saviors. Mentors are advocates, advisers, and role models. You do not need a degree in psychology or hours of special training to be a mentor. All that is required is the commitment to make a difference, the willingness to listen and hear, and the discipline to balance your heart and your mind.

When you give of your time, experience, and wisdom to a young person, you are sowing the seeds of pride, confidence, and accomplishment. And there is no greater joy and satisfaction than seeing those seeds grow and blossom.

Mentoring is about the future. It is about changing the world by opening it up for young people. Help a child to dream and to believe in his or her dream, and you help create hope in place of fear, self-esteem in place of doubt, ambition in place of powerlessness. Help a young person to fulfill his or her potential, and you create a legacy of hope that will be passed on from generation to generation.

The Gift of Mentoring

The question people ask most often about mentoring is, "How do you find the time?" The answer is simple—you *make* time.

A young man I worked with once confided in me that he felt unfulfilled in his life despite having a beautiful family, a promising career, and financial security.

"Have you thought of giving some of your time to kids in the community?" I asked.

"I can find the time, Tommy," he said softly, "but I am afraid I wouldn't have anything else to give them."

Here was a man who was making it but could not embrace his success. When you choose to become a mentor to a young person, you must first acknowledge that you are worth the admiration of that young person, that yours is an example worth imitating. That is the gift you give yourself when you decide to share your time, your love, your experience, and your trust as a mentor.

"I get an incredible sense of satisfaction from working with young people," says Houston Mills, a member of our Louisville, Kentucky, chapter and the Black Airline Pilots Association. "God gave me a vision about the beauty and sanctity of life for each one of us, and I am duplicating that vision and passing it on to others, especially our children. It's part of the legacy I would like to leave behind."

That is the personal reward of mentoring that draws such noted people as Hank Aaron, Mayor Dennis Archer of Detroit, Mayor Bill Campbell of Atlanta, Kenneth Chenault, Dr. Johnetta Cole, Bill Cosby, Sal Diaz-Verson, George Fraser, Danny Glover, Earl Graves, Dorothy Height, Maynard Jackson, Ingrid Sanders Jones, John Lewis, Dennis Malamatinas, Nelson Mandela, Kweisi Mfume, U.S. Senator Sam Nunn, Richard Parsons, Colin Powell, Dr. Jane Smith, Denzel Washington, and Andrew Young.

You might be surprised to read that such prominent, busy people make time to mentor. But as you will hear some of them recount in their own words, every one of us, no matter how successful and accomplished, reaches a point when professional and material achievements are not enough and we want to experience a deeper sense of satisfaction. Mentoring is a way to find such fulfillment by building your personal legacy for the future.

Most important, however, is that mentoring works. A recent study of the Big Brothers/Big Sisters national mentoring program found that young people who met with a mentor three times a month for one year were 46 percent less likely to begin using illegal drugs, 52 percent less likely to skip school, and 33 percent less likely to get into fights. In addition, students with mentors were shown to have greater confidence in their performance at school and better relations with their family.

In another study, Proctor & Gamble looked at its mentoring programs in the Cincinnati school system and found that the participating young people were more likely to stay in school, achieve and aspire to better grades, and pursue a higher education. Before the mentoring programs were instituted, only 25 to 30 percent of students from the schools involved with Proctor & Gamble continued their education after graduation; after mentoring, 86 percent of the senior classes went on to college.

Mentoring is a renewable resource—it doesn't stop when the individual relationship is over. Young people are affected by their mentors throughout their entire lives and most likely end up mentoring others. Mentoring is, in a very real sense, a two-way empowerment. The mentee gains a role model and looks to the mentor for guidance in becoming a better young adult. In return, the mentor gains a youthful perspective from the mentee, which adds to the mentor's personal development.

Mentoring is a gift you and the person you mentor share. And it is a gift that keeps on giving.

Mentoring the 100 Way

Traditionally, mentoring has been defined as a one-on-one relationship between a youth and an adult. It is the process of sharing personal knowledge and providing consistent reassurance to help a young person cope with the diverse and challenging situations in his life.

Every community throughout the country has its own specific resources and needs. Therefore, in an effort to maximize the 100 Black Men of America's mentoring capability, we decided to expand the traditional one-on-one mentoring programs to include group mentoring as an alternate yet effective way to influence young people. However, the focus of the mentoring process remains identical: to have mentees gain the confidence they need in order to become responsible for their own future and to help them develop their academic and occupational skills.

Children learn by observing and imitating adults. Or as we say in the 100 Black Men of America: "What they see is what they'll be." And so we have an obligation to offer them positive role models. "Mentoring the 100 way," explains Houston Mills, "is showing kids how to replicate success. Not just material success but total success in their lives."

This is particularly resonant for us in the 100. We are very aware of the fact that we are the first generation of African Americans who have access to the opportunities—in education, careers, politics—that we have enjoyed. As such, we feel that we have a special obligation to serve as role models for the youth of our community.

The 100 Black Men of America, Inc., got its start in New York in the early 1960s. Influential black leaders including Robert Magnum, James Dumpson, and Kenneth Clarke began meeting to form an organization that could constructively strengthen cooperation among blacks. The idea was to find a base from which they could address and influence the real overriding issues facing the black community.

The One Hundred Men was formally organized in 1963. The founders—including also former New York Mayor David Dinkins, the Honorable Herbert Evans, the Honorable James W. Watson, to name a few—consisted of a group of African American lawyers, physicians, educators, civic leaders, entrepreneurs, and government leaders. The group's first president was Robert Magnum, one of the first black deputy police commissioners in New York City and later a New York State judge.

"The idea was that a group of black men who had been able to achieve some modicum of success in society would unite to work more effectively for the black community," explains New York attorney Godfrey Murrain, who was the general counsel and secretary of the organization for many years and the founder of the Scholarship

Committee. "Our primary purpose was and remains to improve the quality of life of African Americans and the African American community."

Eventually, the name of the group was changed to One Hundred Black Men. Following the New York model, groups soon formed in New Jersey and Long Island. By 1986, there were nine chapters. That year, at a national conference held in Atlanta, Georgia, the 100 Black Men of America, Inc., was founded.

Today, the organization has more than 10,000 members in 93 chapters throughout the country and four international chapters. We are comprised of African American men who work in business, industry, public affairs, education, professional sports, and government. Although mentoring is the cornerstone of our organization, we also sponsor programs and awareness campaigns in such areas as education, health and wellness, and economic development that reach some 20 million individuals annually.

The members of the 100 currently mentor more than 120,000 young men and women each year directly through the work of our individual chapters. Thousands more are mentored through our partnerships with corporations and government agencies such as Aetna Financial Services, Allstate, AmeriCorp, Anheuser Busch Co., Bank of America, Browning Ferris Industries (BFI), Burger King, Carson Products Co., Chubbs, City of Atlanta, Coca-Cola, Coors Brewing Co., Delta Air Lines, First Union National Bank, Fulton County Government, General Motors, Hyatt Hotels, HUD, McDonald's, Miller Brewing Company, Nike, Paine Webber, State Farm, UPS, U.S. Centers for Disease Control and Prevention, U.S. Department of Health and Human Services, U.S. Department of Justice, U.S. Department of Labor, U.S. Office of National Drug Control Policy, The Village Foundation, and W. H. Smith Co.

"Our mentoring programs are now recognized nationally as models of success, because we use a very rigorous training and evaluation system," explains Dr. Joshua W. Murfree, Jr., National Mentoring Chairman of the 100. "Mentoring the 100 way is *SMART* mentoring. Each chapter is encouraged to be flexible and creative in identifying *Specific* groups of young people in its local area who it considers would benefit from mentoring. We insist on *Measurable* outcomes to show that we are making a difference. We set *Attainable* and *Realistic* goals. We develop each mentoring program with its specific *Target* population in mind.

"The result is that we have a wide variety of mentoring programs that are designed to meet the needs of the young people of each of our chapters' community. They range from 'Barbershop 101,' a program that gives young people a chance to learn about life with older folks in a relaxed, home-town setting, to the new five-hundred-acre, state-of-the-art youth leadership institute in metro Atlanta donated by Browning Ferris Industries (BFI) and due to be completed in 2001."

Mentoring is now recognized as the cutting-edge social investment strategy for the twenty-first century. For example, the Clinton administration allocated hundreds of millions of dollars in its budget for mentoring programs; the W. K. Kellogg Foundation recently gave millions of dollars to organizations that provide mentoring for African American men and boys; and the U.S. Office of National Drug Control Policy under the dynamic leadership of General Barry McCafrey earmarked a significant portion of its $17 billion budget for mentoring initiatives.

I have dedicated myself to mentoring because I want to help teach our young people the values and beliefs that have served me well in my life and to help them avoid the mistakes I have seen myself and my friends make. My work with the 100 Black Men of America has given me the opportunity both to mentor one-on-one and to bring mentoring into the lives of hundreds of thousands of young men and women by tapping into our members' vast network of goodwill and resources.

I have never forgotten the lesson I learned at the barbershop in Toccoa: to serve my community and be responsible for and accountable to the next generation. The men in the barbershop of my childhood were people who believed in me and cared about me. And it feels good to know that they would be proud of me and the mentoring work we at the 100 Black Men of America are doing.

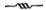

This book will provide sensible, practical advice on all aspects of mentoring based on the successful experience of the 100's extensive national network of mentoring programs. It will cover such topics as understanding the do's and don'ts of successful mentoring; building the mentoring relationship; choosing a mentoring program that is right for you; developing programs for young people in schools, neighborhoods, and workplaces; and partnering with businesses, corporations, educational institutions, and nonprofit organizations to expand the mentoring experience. In addition, to help you get started with your mentoring experience, a comprehensive resource directory of national and local nonprofit, community, and corporate mentoring programs—including program descriptions, addresses, telephone numbers, and Internet connections—is included at the end of the book.

I am nourished and filled with joy by those special smiles that I get from kids whose lives I have touched through mentoring. Those smiles that say: "Hey, you'll see, someday you'll be proud of me."

It is my profound wish that this book will help you experience that same pride, joy, and sense of fulfillment through the miracles of mentoring.

CHAPTER ONE

Real Men Giving Real Time: Mentoring the 100 Way

Man shall not live by bread alone. Man must live by faith—faith in himself and faith in others.

—DR. BENJAMIN E. MAYS

I was born up north—northern Georgia, that is—in 1950. About seven miles south of the South Carolina state line, Toccoa, my hometown, was a quiet little place of about 18,000 people. With acres and acres of woodlands and the beautiful Toccoa Falls, it felt like it was "God's country."

Most people had jobs at the foundry or the furniture factory or owned their own businesses.

Blacks made up about 10 percent of the population and we lived in a tight-knit community, with our own stores, restaurants, churches, and schools. The creek that separated our part of town from the white section ran through the back of my parents' property, and my friends and I often leaped across to play with the white kids or they crossed to play with us.

Somehow, in spite of the signs that read FOR WHITES ONLY and NO COLOREDS and the fact that we could only get served at the back door of some places in town, we did not have the sense that we were inferior. I remember going to the movies on Saturday nights and thinking that we were lucky to be sitting up in the balcony—the section designated for blacks—because there was no one above us who might accidentally spill soda pop on our heads or throw their candy wrappers over the railing.

It was not that we were blind to the injustice of segregation or immune to the hurt and the anger it caused—it was that we were not poisoned by feelings of inferiority and powerlessness. Yes, it was painful and frightening to drive through an all-white county on the way to a basketball game and see the words NIGGER, DON'T LET THE SUN SET ON YOUR BLACK BEHIND scrawled in red paint on boards and fences along the road, but we had been taught by our elders that the ugliness lay not in us but in the person who had written those words.

The adults in the community were like a security blanket wrapped around us. They might have had their own personal anger or bitterness, but they never passed it on to us kids. My mother—a wise philosopher—used to say, "There are those of your color who are not of your kind, and those of your kind who are not of your color. You've got to judge people on the basis of their character, not their skin."

The black community of Toccoa was really a village looking out for its own. The adults were concerned that the young people should do the best they could, and each one of them played a part in making sure they would. Our parents, teachers, community, and religious leaders instilled in us a sense of self-pride—if we worked hard, we could do anything.

I knew that I had to work twice or maybe three times as hard to get where I wanted to go in life. But that did not make me think that I could not get to where I was heading. It was not important that our desks were not as new as the ones in the white school or that our books were tattered. We were in the classroom to learn, and we had teachers who cared about us and gave us everything they had. It was thanks to them that in 1968 I graduated salutatorian of the last segregated class of Whitman Street High School and went on to Fort Valley State University—a historically black university that wanted me for my mind, not my ball playing ability, as was common for larger institutions.

Our elders taught us by example. They came together as a community to make their voices heard politically and economically. I learned many important lessons about the power of coalitions and the mighty dollar as I helped pass out election fliers and listened to my father and other community leaders talk about collective action. They were my inspiration as I became president of the student government at Fort Valley and then got involved in local and national politics.

And let me tell you, I was so filled with pride when I returned years later to that same county in Georgia where I had been warned as a high school student to not let the sun set on my behind. Here I was, one of Georgia U.S. Senator Sam Nunn's chief aides, called in to help resolve racial tensions following a local civil rights demonstration. I brought everything my community had taught me to that negotiating table and celebrated the moment not only as a personal validation but also as a victory for that whole village that helped raise me.

The elders of Toccoa had all suffered the injustices of Jim Crow, but they recognized that every challenge is an opportunity. They taught us that the courage to face great challenges creates great warriors. And they encouraged us to go after our dreams with great courage. If the front door is locked, they would tell us, go around to the back. And if the back door is locked, get in through the window. But most important, once you get in, open the door for those following you and help them in.

It is this way of looking at the challenges we faced as African Americans that shaped my generation. We were encouraged to seize the opportunities that the Civil Rights movement was creating. We were taught to make opportunities for ourselves and for others. It is this approach to creating social change that is the guiding principle of the 100 Black Men of America, Inc.

"If you look at the members of the 100," says Lenny Springs, senior vice president of First Union Bank and the founding president of our Charlotte, North Carolina, chapter, "someone in their lives recognized them and told them they could achieve and be someone if they believed in themselves. I know people did that for me. I can't forget that. I won't forget that. I give back because someone paved the way for me."

That is what the 100 is all about: real men giving real time. The way was paved for us by our parents, our teachers, our mentors, our ancestors. It was paved by the people who gave their hearts and their lives to demand for African Americans the human rights guaranteed to all Americans by the Constitution. We have not forgotten. We will not forget. And we will give everything we have to pass on to our children and the generations to come the courage to become great warriors by helping them make opportunities of the challenges they face.

In the Time of Struggle, a Blueprint for Success

"I have a dream," Dr. Martin Luther King, Jr., proclaimed from the steps of the Lincoln Memorial on August 28, 1963, "that my four little children will one day live in a nation where they will not be judged by the color of their skins, but by the content of their character."

As Dr. King addressed these historic words to the 200,000 people who had gathered in the Tidal Basin at the climax of the March on Washington—the largest rally of the civil rights era—the One Hundred Black Men were making a difference in New York City. The organization's founders were of the strong belief that in order to ensure the long-term success of the struggle for civil rights, African American youth had to be ready to make the most of the opportunities that would be created by the movement. They recognized very early on that they would have to redefine the concept of a "village." And in order to do so, they went about building coalitions, partnerships, and a broad base of support to focus a tremendous amount of resources on youth development. They came to embody Ralph Ellison's philosophy that "democracy is a collectivity of individuals."

The 100 is now 10,000 strong. Our volunteer members give openly and generously of their time, their energy, and their hearts. They do so because they know each of them has beaten the odds and it is their obligation to stay true to the civil rights motto of "each one teach one, each one reach one."

Our membership includes, along with many others, such distinguished men as:

- Hank Aaron, Baseball's Home Run King
- Dennis Archer, Mayor, City of Detroit
- Bill Campbell, Mayor, City of Atlanta
- Kenneth Chennault, President, American Express
- Johnnie Cochran, Attorney
- Bill Cosby, Philanthropist and Entertainer
- Earl Graves, Publisher and CEO of Black Enterprise Magazine
- Richard Parsons, President, Time Warner
- Honorable P. J. Patterson, Prime Minister of Jamaica
- John Lewis, U.S. Congressman
- Kweisi Mfume, President and CEO, NAACP
- Alonzo Mourning, Miami Heat of the NBA
- Colin Powell, Retired Chairman, Joint Chiefs of Staff

- Andrew Young, Former Ambassador
- Carl Ware, President, Coca-Cola

My good friend Ron Williams, former director of diversity for Nike, puts it best: "The people who make a real difference in this world are the ones that do not take a seat but take a stand. And the 100 takes a stand for young people." And we do that by continuing to expand on the concept of collective responsibility.

We are building a new kind of village. Its streets may exist only in our imaginations and its barber shops may exist only in our hearts, but its support for our children is as real and powerful as that of the Toccoa of my childhood.

Mentoring the 100 Way

"Everybody can be great. Because anybody can serve," said Dr. Martin Luther King, Jr. "You don't have to have a college degree to serve. You don't have to make your subject and your verb agree to serve. You don't have to know about Plato and Aristotle to serve. You don't have to know Einstein's theory of relativity to serve. You only need a heart full of grace. A soul generated by love."

Mentoring young people is a way to be great. It is a way to create miracles for our children and ourselves. These miracles are as basic and fundamental as seeing a child grow and flourish and making room for a young person in your heart and in your life. The miracles of mentoring are tangible, as you see the mentee:

- Develop respect for him- or herself and the mentor.
- Develop positive lifelong goals.

- Become excited about activities with the mentor.
- Develop a strong personal relationship with the mentor.
- View the mentor as a role model.
- Pursue higher education.
- Look to the mentor for guidance and direction.
- Become good friends with the mentor.
- Discover his or her personal spirituality.
- Expand the mentor relationship to include his or her family.

"Nobody will think you're somebody," the traditional saying goes, "if you don't think so yourself." A 16-year-old from Charlotte, North Carolina, sure did not think he was somebody. He did not even think that he would live to see his twenty-first birthday. But that was before he met Lenny Springs of our Charlotte chapter.

Lenny and his mentee were matched up by the mentoring program that the chapter runs for school children in the community. Lenny, an experienced and dedicated mentor, encouraged his mentee to think beyond the violence and hopelessness of his immediate surroundings, to dream, and to set goals for himself. Slowly, the young man's grades soon began to improve. He started showing signs of becoming less guarded, he sounded more hopeful.

But after about 11 months, Lenny's mentee dropped out of sight. "I thought we had lost him," recalls Lenny. "But a couple of years later, I stopped at a McDonald's for lunch, and there he was, all grown up, the manager of the restaurant. And not only that, he was putting himself through North Carolina State College, majoring in business administration. He told me how much he truly appreciated my help and support during the hard times. He thanked me for caring. I can't tell you what it's like to hear that I've had such an impact on the life of a young man.

"I knew then and there that mentoring is an act of faith. You just have to do the best you can and hope you sow the seeds of success. I am sure that one day I am going to look up and see a President of the United States who was mentored by the 100."

"Mentoring the 100 Way" is a holistic approach to empowering children to realize their full potential and develop the self-esteem needed for success and personal fulfillment. Our mentoring programs are conducted on a consistent, ongoing, and reinforced basis, encouraging both mentors and mentees alike to engage in the mentoring relationship by providing resources, moral support, and guidance. We also establish specific goals for the mentee, such as improving school performance, learning computer skills, or managing social interactions.

Our members receive extensive training and support through our National Mentoring Chairman and regional coordinators. In addition to a national curriculum and train-the-trainer workshops, the 100 has a unique certification process through Clark-Atlanta University where mentors can keep abreast of new techniques and information in the world of mentoring.

Every one of our chapters has a mentoring program; many have more than one. The programs vary widely, each designed to meet the needs of the young people in the chapter's community. The 100 maintains an electronic reporting system that provides information on the full extent of our mentoring programs. This reporting system ensures that the national office has accurate quarterly information about the number of young people involved in the different programs and allows the local chapters to exchange information about their various mentoring initiatives.

"Mentoring the 100 Way" endeavors to bring hope into the lives of young people, to empower them to dream and to go after their dreams. What each of the mentoring programs share, however, is the dedication of our members to give children the encouragement, guidance, and support they need to grow, become independent, and reach their full potential.

Project Success

When we started the Atlanta chapter in 1986, we wanted to make a major statement to the city about being involved in the community, about mentoring and working with young people. We decided that we would adopt a class to mentor—a group of students from a school in one of Atlanta's troubled inner-city neighborhoods. We specifically looked for a school and a community where we could make the biggest difference. We met with the superintendent of public schools, and he recommended that we go into Archer High School in the Perry Homes neighborhood.

Now, you have to understand the Perry Homes area. It is one of the toughest, economically challenged public housing projects in the country. Several years ago, at the height of Atlanta's drug epidemic, the mayor and the chairman of the Fulton County Commission, along with several other government officials, went there to spend the night to experience firsthand what the environment was like. Halfway through the night, in spite of the fact that there were all these police officers with the delegation, a gunfight between rival drug dealers erupted within a couple of blocks of Perry Homes. The police rushed in and moved them out of the neighborhood. That was all they could do.

So it is no surprise that Archer High School was one of the worst in the city in terms of academic performance. At that time, of all the students who started eighth grade, only 43 percent graduated from high school. And out of those who graduated each year, only about 15 students went on to college. Just think, out of a whole community, only 15 children were able to believe in their future.

The 100 Black Men of Atlanta knew that Archer High was the place for us to launch Project Success. We picked an eighth-grade class at random and got to work. I still remember the first day we went to meet the kids. There were 35 of them, boys and girls, some tough, others shy, a few clowning around, a couple totally disengaged. The members of the 100 went around the room and introduced ourselves, describing the kind of work each one of us did, and explaining what we wanted to achieve by being part of this mentoring program. Then, we asked the students to introduce themselves and say what they wanted to do after graduating high school. There were lots of sullen "don't knows." There were girls who wanted to be models and guys who wanted to play pro ball and be rap stars.

And then we got to one young lady who said: "My name is Sonya Jelks, and I think all of you are crazy if you think you are going to be MCs or anything like that. What I want is to go to school and become an executive secretary."

Here was a 13-year-old smart enough to know that not everyone can be a celebrity. This young lady was ambitious enough to want to do something with her life, and realistic enough to see that an education is an important part of success. Yet her goals were determined by her limited view of the world, not by her dreams. She wanted to be somebody, but she also believed that there were few options available to her.

I knew at that moment what mentoring was about: We wanted to show Sonya and all of the kids in that class—all of our students—that a world of options is available to them. We wanted to engender in them the same feelings of pride and offer the same kind of support that we got from the elders in our community when we were growing up.

The members of our chapter had to work hard to accomplish this. The kids we were mentoring came from an environment that severely restricted their experience and outlook on life. To give you a small but telling example, these kids lived right near the downtown area, with its glass and concrete office towers, and yet many of them had never been inside one of those buildings, not even simply to look around. So our task was to motivate them to perform well academically and to expose them to a variety of new experiences.

We began by offering them a written contract that guaranteed that if they got into college, the 100 would pay the full cost of their tuition. Within 90 days of signing these contracts, their grades were up by 23 percent. And we were there every step of the way. At least three of us went to the school every week. We would take the students on field trips to different companies and small businesses in the city, visit local colleges and museums, attend concerts and plays.

Toward the end of the first year, it was clear we were succeeding. The kids performed well above others in their class. But it was not until that year's annual 100 Black Men of America, Inc., national gala that I realized the degree to which we had touched these young people's lives.

I knew it was going to be a great night. All of us in the Atlanta chapter were looking forward to showing off our accomplishments to the whole community. But nothing could have prepared me for what happened. Instead of the kids I was expecting—35 boys and girls I had gotten to know so well—35 beautiful, beaming young men and women in tuxedos and evening gowns arrived at the ballroom. As we watched them walk in—excited, proud, a little nervous—we members of the 100 Atlanta Chapter were all overwhelmed. These young people, the most ambitious of whom had wanted to become an executive secretary, carried themselves like people who knew they were going places. And I knew that I had helped them see that they had some place to go. I was so proud, I could have popped my buttons.

At that moment, I experienced one of the miracles of mentoring: I realized that mentoring is not just a project you are involved in but that you are transforming a young person's life. It is just such moments of intense emotional satisfaction that keep high-powered, busy people involved in mentoring year after year.

We continued to mentor those 35 kids for the next four years. By the beginning of their junior year, it became clear that even though they were doing well compared to the rest of the school, they were not quite ready to go to college. So we intensified our efforts. In cooperation with Atlanta Metropolitan College, we created a Saturday Academy. Every Saturday, the students went to classes to supplement their math and English skills and to prepare for college entrance exams. We worked with them. We even paid them a minimum wage stipend, so that they would not have to miss the Saturday session in order to hold down a job.

At the end of their senior year, 33 out of 35 students in that class graduated. Of the two who didn't, one was a young man who proved to be a hard case. We even had the mayor talk to him, but he simply would not change and ended up in jail. The other one was a young lady who got pregnant. But we helped her return to school, and she eventually went on to graduate. So ultimately, 97 percent of that class graduated, compared with 43 percent for the rest of the school.

Not only did most of our students graduate from high school, 27 went on to college and three to trade school. And the bottom line to all of this is that we didn't do anything magical. We simply *encouraged* these young women and men. We *believed* in them. We were there for them consistently, and we motivated them to strive for more. We also let them know that we would continue to support them as they worked toward their dreams.

Most important, we helped them define success for themselves. Success is not a destination, it is a journey. A mentor's responsibility is to guide young people along their individual paths.

And with encouragement, support, and guidance, kids will dream great dreams and, in the process, become great. Take Sonya, for example, the young lady who started out wanting to be an executive secretary. She graduated from Syracuse University with a degree in management information systems and anthropology, and a 3.6 grade point average. She went on to get her Master's degree a year later and is now an executive with a Fortune 500 company. At the moment, she is trying to decide whether to go to law school or to get her Ph.D. The world might have lost a great executive secretary, but instead we got a young woman who knows that there is no limit to what she can accomplish. That is the miracle of mentoring: It gives children the keys to the world.

Project Success is now in its fourteenth year. Its alumnae have gone on to graduate from such prestigious institutions as Voorhees College, Syracuse University, Spelman College, Georgia Institute of Technology, Clark-Atlanta University, and Florida A & M University. The truly gratifying thing is that they are also now giving back to the community, mentoring a new generation of young people to follow in their footsteps.

Our West Texas chapter has a successful program that helps young boys make the transition into adulthood.

" 'Rites of Passage' is based on African traditions of initiation into manhood," explains R. D. Johnson, president of the West Texas chapter of the 100, located in Lubbock. "You say initiation or rites of passage, and often people will ask, 'What do you do, take them into the woods and make them walk on coals and pound drums?' But that is just ignorant. It is pretending like all of us do not have to be initiated into how things really are done when we enter into the adult world.

"We usually have between twenty and thirty boys in the program, ranging in age from nine to sixteen. Every Saturday we get together with the kids at a neighborhood center for two hours. We engage them as a group and talk about one of the seven basic principles the program focuses on: spirituality, family, etiquette, African American history, life skills, violence prevention, and inner resources.

"We encourage the kids to think about what it means to be a man, about the responsibility that carries. And we help them to start to develop the tools they will need to do the job well.

"We start by talking about self-definition. It is simple stuff like writing down five things you are good at—like throwing a ball, or spelling, or computers. You should see the looks on the boys' faces when they read those lists out loud. 'Man,' they say, 'I didn't know I could do so many things this well.'

"We talk about the history of our people. The schools do not teach African American history. So for the kids to hear about all the amazing things our ancestors have done, it is really an eye-opening experience. It helps them see themselves in a different light. I remember a while back we were talking about the Tuskegee Airmen, and this one kid just could not believe it. 'There were black pilots?' he kept asking. 'For real?' Somehow, that just captured his imagination. Well, you should have been there when he heard that a black astronaut, Ronald McNair, was the first man to play saxophone in space. He just burst out laughing."

R. D. Johnson says that he derives a great sense of gratification from mentoring. "I was raised by my mother so I know the emotional burdens and pitfalls of growing up without a father. My mother did a great job, but it is not the same. There is a real piece missing for a boy who has no man in the house to look up to and learn from.

"I was also mentored by the principal of my school and the leader of my Boy Scout troop. The two of them did a great deal for me, and what I am doing now to a large extent is repaying that debt.

"I carried a lot of resentment for a long time about not

having a father. I know what it is like to really need that male presence in your life. So I get a tremendous charge out of giving boys an opportunity to be mentored along their journey to becoming men. That is why I have a special place in my heart for our 'Rites of Passage' program.

"Initiation to the ways of the world takes many forms. I remember the first time I went out to dinner at a fancy restaurant. I didn't know which fork to use or how to address the waiter. It was embarrassing. And there is no reason for that. All you need is someone to show you. So that is one of the things we do. We take the kids to good restaurants and we model for them how you conduct yourself at a business meal or a celebration. They love it, soaking it all up like sponges.

"We also arrange outings to museums and concerts. We go to ball games and on fishing trips; we bring them into work environments and into houses of worship. And all the time, we help them put the experiences into the perspective of their passage into manhood.

"It is events like those that you look to experience as a mentor, to connect to something that is meaningful to the kids. We take the same tack no matter what it is that we are talking about, whether it is health and sexuality, family relationships, career planning, you name it. You have to give the kids a framework and then expose them to lots of different experiences and people."

R. D. Johnson believes that this kind of group mentoring truly works for the members of his chapter. "We are a community of men—our own little village," he explains. "We provide the kids the guidance they need, and we give each other the support we need to live up to this responsibility. But don't get me wrong, it is tough sometimes.

There are challenges. We make mistakes. There are some kids you just can't reach. There are those you lose.

"When you connect with your mentee, however, it is a feeling like no other. Once the trust is there, you can get deeper. You spend more time together and you find your mentee starting to open up. When it's just the two of you, he'll talk about stuff that might be uncomfortable to bring up in a group. (Like family problems, girls, and real private dreams.) That is when you get the opportunity to really help shape a young man's life. That is when you become a real role model.

"Your own kids, they are sort of stuck with you. So it is hard for them to see you as a role model, especially for an adolescent who is trying to be independent. But a kid who is looking to be mentored is hungry for that kind of adult presence in his life. It is a real gift to be invited to play that role for a young person."

There is a Jamaican proverb that says that the best passion is compassion. Members of the 100 say over and over again that mentoring young people enriches their lives in so many different ways, as it has for the men of the West Texas chapter, who find the passion they need to lead full, satisfying lives by opening their hearts to kids who need an adult's guiding hand, empathetic ear, and compassionate soul.

Education, Scholarship, and Economic Development

"Education is our passport to the future," wrote Malcolm X, "for tomorrow belongs to the people who prepare for it today." We at the 100 Black Men of America, Inc., are committed to helping our young people pursue their goals and dreams. By the year 2005, more than half of all the people entering the workforce will be minorities. At the same time, one-half of all jobs will require a higher level of education and technological training. Our mentoring programs are designed not only to create well-grounded, emotionally secure young people but also to challenge them to be competitive in the current marketplace.

In addition to service learning programs and a host of other educational initiatives, the 100 Black Men of America, Inc., provides financial support in the form of scholarships to help young people take advantage of educational opportunities. In 1997, for example, we dispersed $200,000 in scholarships out of a $1,000,000 portfolio of funds provided by such longtime supporters as the McDonald's Corporation, Carson Products, and the Coca-Cola Foundation.

Our national scholarship recipients attend such distinguished institutions as: Alabama A & M, Baruch College, Delaware State, Delta State University, Florida A & M, Florida State University, Georgia State, Georgia Tech, Hampton University, Harvard University, Howard University, Jackson State University, Morehouse College, Morgan State University, Old Dominion University, Penn State University, Pratt University, Polytechnic University, Spelman College, Tennessee State, Tuskegee University, University of Maryland, University of Michigan, University of Tennessee, University of Virginia, Valdosta State University, Vanderbilt University, Xavier, and Yale University.

Oprah Winfrey likes to say that "luck is a matter of preparation meeting opportunity." The 100 Black Men of America, Inc., is dedicated to giving young people every opportunity to prepare for success. But we also understand that economic empowerment and self-esteem go hand in hand—they are inseparable. In fact, achieving economic prosperity is a major step toward self-determination for our young people and our community. Our mentoring program remains committed, therefore, to developing programs that also prepare our children to go from the classroom to the boardroom.

The elders of Toccoa have been my lifelong inspiration. They managed to provide us children with a sense of pride and self-worth in the face of discrimination, prejudice, and economic challenges. Most of all, they gave us a sense of belonging to a community that cared about our future. They helped us to see that real solutions lie in hard work and success, not in anger and violence. Now it is our turn—our obligation—to give the next generation these same tools and support.

The late educator Dr. Benjamin Mays, who was one of the most illustrious members of the 100 Black Men of America, wrote:

> The tragedy in life does not lie in not reaching your goal. The tragedy lies in having no goal to reach. It isn't a calamity not to die with dreams unfulfilled, but it is a calamity not to dream. . . . It is not a disgrace not to reach the stars, but it is a disgrace to have no stars to reach for. Not failure, but low aim is the sin.

Dr. Mays's words are at the heart of the mentoring approach of the 100 Black Men of America. We do not believe that there are children who are at risk of failure. We believe that there are children who are born into environments that put them at risk of not dreaming. And when children do not dream, no matter what their socioeconomic background is, their future—and ours—is at risk.

What You Can Do:

1. Decide for yourself if you want to invest in the future by mentoring a young person.
2. Seek out a mentoring program that meets your needs.
3. Make a serious commitment to mentor and stick to it.

CHAPTER TWO

Is Mentoring for You? Questions to Consider Before You Start

We all have ability. The difference is how we use it.

—STEVIE WONDER

You don't need any special skills to mentor. No advanced degrees or impressive résumés are required for making a difference in a young person's life. Honorific titles, fat bank accounts, and well-tailored clothes are no guarantee that you will make a good mentor. On the other hand, motivation, empathy, commitment, and flexibility will make it possible for you to enter a child's world and lovingly establish yourself as a trusted guide, a valued advisor, a cherished role model.

The questions in this chapter are designed to help you think about the responsibilities of a mentor and about the skills, attitudes, expectations, and limitations you would bring to a mentoring relationship. It is my hope that they will not discourage you from becoming a mentor but rather encourage you to be realistically enthusiastic about working with young people. However, if after reading the chapter you do find yourself disinclined to mentor, if you feel you're not yet ready for a one-on-one mentoring relationship with a child, do not despair. Find another way to make a difference in the life of a child. Coach a sports team, get involved in a literacy program, or become active in a community organization that works with young people. And when the time is right, you can start considering mentoring once again.

1. Do You Enjoy Spending Time with Children?

This might seem like an odd question to ask of someone who is reading a book on mentoring young people, but it is essential that you seriously consider what it would be like for you to spend several hours each month with a child or a group of children. Kids—especially kids who come from challenging family environments—are extremely sensitive to how other people feel about them. They will know if you do not enjoy being with them and will feel rejected.

And let's face it, if you're not getting some satisfaction out of the relationship, chances are you're not going to stick with it.

"I found mentoring too difficult," says Carol, a medical writer who participated in a community-based mentoring program in San Francisco. "There was no reward for all my efforts. It felt like my mentee just wanted me to take her places and buy her things. Like it was all about money.

"Rosie and I kind of got started on the wrong foot. I thought we would kick things off in style, so I took her to a concert and a really nice dinner for our first outing together. But all she talked about was how much the tickets must have cost and how expensive the food was. I just didn't know how to get her interested in anything else. And I got so frustrated."

What Carol did not realize is how big a deal it was for her mentee to be out "in style." She interpreted Rosie's fascination with this new experience as a sign of selfishness rather than as the natural curiosity of a child about a world she probably had not seen before. Had Carol been more prepared to delight in the unabashed ways in which kids can express their needs, wants, and feelings, she may have been able to channel Rosie's interest in how much things cost into a discussion of careers, finances, or family history.

A successful mentor can turn any experience into a learning opportunity. However, to do so, you have to genuinely enjoy children and be open and sensitive to their ways of perceiving and interpreting the world.

"I get a real good feeling from the kids," says Lonnie J. Carr, general superintendent of MARTA in Atlanta and vice president of finance for the 100 Black Men of America, Inc. "Working with them takes away the stress of the day. It did not start out like that for me. I got involved in the 100 back in 1991, when I was still living in Baltimore, because I liked the organization's mission of working with African American youth.

"I decided to try one-on-one mentoring, went through the training, and was matched up with a young man in middle school. I've got to tell you, that was one of the toughest things I've ever had to do. The responsibility of taking on a kid's life just felt overwhelming. After a couple of months, I knew that I wasn't doing anybody any good by sticking with it. The program assigned the boy another mentor, and I took a little time to reflect.

"But even after this difficult experience, I felt the urge to be around kids. So I tried my hand at group mentoring and started going to our Saturday Academy, a structured weekend tutorial and life skills enhancement program. Every Saturday, a group of us men would help the young people who would come in for extra help with their schoolwork. Well, that was great. There was more structure, more support. I couldn't wait for the weekends to roll around. I loved the smiles on the kids' faces when they learned something new or finally mastered a task that was giving them trouble. I felt recharged every time I went.

"I stuck with group mentoring for a long time. But gradually, I built up enough confidence to start mentoring one on one. I became involved with a promising but challenging young man, and we soon developed a terrific relationship. I got an even deeper satisfaction from the time we spent together than I would have years ago, but I was in a different place in my life. It is a real gift to be able to share an important part of another person's life, especially a young man or woman who truly needs a source of stability from an attentive and sympathetic adult."

2. What Is It You Want to Get Out of Mentoring?

Dijuan S. Kellom, a freshman at Morehouse College and executive director of the Collegiate 100 of the Atlanta chapter of the 100 Black Men of America, says, "My advice to a potential mentor is to do it only if your heart is really in it.

"I have had mentors since I came to Atlanta when I was fourteen. The 100 had a program at my school, and they have been mentoring me ever since. The thing that was so amazing to me, that really made me understand mentoring, was that these guys were doing it because they wanted to—not because they had to. As a kid, that makes you feel really special. Here are men, taking the time to show you what's what because they truly care.

"I now mentor high school kids because I know how much having a mentor has helped me. I want to pay back and to make a difference in my own right."

Making a difference in a young life is what mentoring is all about. The opportunity to do so is all the reward a true mentor asks for. You should not do it to get a promotion, or to secure a lucrative contract, or to gain public office, or to have your name in lights, or even to get another award plaque to hang in your office.

However, if sharing a bag of fries and a long walk with a nine-year-old is your idea of a great afternoon, you should mentor. If seeing a kid who normally would not ask a question in class deliver her first public speech fills your heart with joy, you should mentor. And if you are brought to tears by hearing a high school senior who once read at the fourth-grade level flawlessly recite a poem by Langston Hughes in front of an audience of 2,500 people, you should mentor.

Mentor from your heart, and your reward will be the lifelong satisfaction of knowing that you helped shape the course of a young person's life. Anything less, and you will be cheating yourself and the hopes of a child.

3. Are You Prepared to Make the Necessary Time Commitment?

Time is a major concern in mentoring. As I have mentioned before, you have to be prepared to commit a few hours every week or every other week. For many people, that seems like an insurmountable hurdle. But ask yourself: Could you find six, or eight, or even ten hours a month for something you really wanted to do? The answer for most of us, no matter how busy, is probably "yes." Mentoring is, after all, a question of setting priorities, not time.

"The time thing, the I-am-too-busy-to-be-a-mentor routine, is usually a convenient way for people not to think about what is really at stake for them if they get involved with a young person," states Randy Walker, mentoring chair of the Metropolitan Detroit chapter of the 100. "I always think of my friend Mike when this question comes up. Mike is a senior vice president with one of the Big Three here in Detroit. As you can imagine, he is a busy man.

" 'I'd love to, Randy, but I'm just too busy,' he would say every time I approached him about mentoring in one of our programs. But I am not one to give up easily. I finally convinced him to come to a Saturday session to talk to the kids about his job for half an hour. 'Are you sure it isn't going to take longer?' Mike kept asking when he showed up at the meeting. 'I've got to get down to the office to finish up a few things.'

"The kids were obviously impressed with Mike. He told them all about the robots used in building cars, about computer design, about satellite navigation. And they kept asking more and more questions about what he did and how he got to be where he is. The next thing I knew, Mike was talking about organizing a trip down to one of his company's plants.

"He ended up spending three hours with the kids that afternoon and we got to tour a plant a few weeks later. But the best part is that a couple of days after that first meeting, Mike called me up and said sort of sheepishly, 'You know Randy, I figured out that I don't need to play golf every week, so is there a way that I could do something with the kids a couple of times a month? I'd really like that.' He has been a mentor ever since. And he is still as busy as ever."

If you have your heart set on being a part of a young person's life, you will find the time. That is how such prominent people as home run king Hank Aaron and Dr. Jane E. Smith, President and CEO of the National Council of Negro Women, stay involved in mentoring.

4. Can You Remain Consistent in Your Commitment?

"Here in the San Francisco and Oakland area," explains Alfred Reynolds of the 100 Black Men of the Northern

California Bay Area, "we have a partnership with the Oakland Unified School District. As part of that, we have adopted the Mary Martin School. It's located in an area of the city that is really economically challenged. Most of the kids come from low-income families. A lot of them are being raised by single parents.

"After our first year at the school, we were evaluating the program when one of the kids, a ninth-grader, became particularly enthusiastic. He kept saying how cool he thought the 100 was. So we asked him what made our program 'cool.' You know what he said? 'We've got lots of people coming and going through here. But you guys keep coming back.'

"I have never forgotten that. You have got to be reliable and consistent. That is what kids look for. They want to know if this person will be there for them in the long run. It basically comes down to a question of trust."

Children, regardless of their socioeconomic environment, are keenly aware of their dependence on adults. They look to us to help them make sense of the world, and they feel helpless and abandoned when we behave in ways that do not make sense to them. It is confusing to a child when an adult fails to live up to a commitment. It is also hurtful. So if you begin mentoring and then stop after a couple of months because you have suddenly gotten busier at work, chances are your mentee will walk away from the experience believing that you lost interest in him or her. And that is the kind of disappointment that lasts a lifetime.

I do not mean to be overly dramatic or to scare anyone away from mentoring. What I am saying is that you have to think long and hard about how this commitment is going to fit into your lifestyle. Can you make some time for a young person every month? The answer has to be "yes," because what is at stake are the hopes, expectations, and self-esteem of a child. There are enough broken promises in the world, and the last thing our children need are drive-by mentors.

5. Are You Prepared for the Challenges of a Mentoring Relationship?

Mentoring is just plain fun. You take your kid to the movies, out to dinner, to a ball game. You share what you know about the world, your interests, your enthusiasms. You get to see life through the eyes of a child, pick up new words, hear new music. You breathe in the vitality of youth and the satisfaction of bringing another person along.

But like any satisfying relationship, mentoring has its challenges and complexities. In the coming chapters, we will talk in more detail about the stages of a mentoring relationship and what you can expect to encounter as you go about building trust, bonding with your mentee, setting mutual goals, and eventually ending the relationship. For the time being, though, ask yourself whether you are prepared to deal with potential challenges such as trouble at school, conflict with parents, differences in values and expectations, questions about drugs and sexuality, tests of your commitment, and so on.

"They are testing you all the time," says Rita, who mentors through an arts-based program in Santa Fe. "I had a real hard time understanding this with my first mentee, Susan. For the first few months, I kept calling and never knew whether she appreciated it or resented it. She never initiated contact, but I just figured I'm the adult, so I plunged ahead.

"I tried to get her involved in small ways. Like if we were going to the movies, I would ask her to call up the theater to find out what time the show started. Responsibilities like that. Yet it seemed that no matter what I did, our relationship never really got to be that close. Susan was a real quiet girl, and I was never able to read her, to know for sure whether I was having any impact on her. It was kind of unnerving and the only thing I could do was to keep believing and moving ahead.

"I was Susan's mentor for a year but we drifted apart and didn't stay in touch. I just figured that I hadn't done such a good job. But then a couple of years ago, I ran into her in a new clothing store that opened up in town. She was working there as a salesperson. It was like I was her favorite aunt, whom she had not seen in a long time. She ran around from behind the counter and hugged me. 'Oh, Rita, it's so good to see you,' she said. 'I can't tell you how grateful I am for everything you did for me.'

"It just goes to show you that you never know what kind of an influence you have on a young person. I ask myself how her life might have been different if I had misinterpreted Susan's behavior and hadn't stayed with her. I compare mentoring to sculpting: The smallest movement can leave a really deep impression."

6. Are You a Good Listener?

"I am in the insurance business," says William Hammond, who is a manager for State Farm Insurance and president of the 100 Black Men of Sonoma County and member of the board of the 100 Black Men of America, "so listening to people is a big part of my job. And I have always thought that I was pretty good at it. But when I started mentoring, I discovered that there was a lot more to listening than I had ever guessed.

"Kids don't just sit down and tell you clearly and directly what's on their minds. You have to pay attention to little things. Their tone of voice, body language, whether they are looking at you or away. I don't mean that you have to go out and get yourself a degree in social work, but you have to learn to listen with your whole body. You have to be in tune to the kind of vibes they are putting out.

"I tell you, mentoring has helped me to become so much better at listening in all aspects of both my personal and professional lives. I have a better relationship with my wife, my kids, my clients, my staff. When you really open up to people and let yourself hear about what's happening for them, it is amazing how people respond."

Listening to people. It seems like such a simple thing. We all do it. But as a mentor, you have to be prepared to listen in an active, involved way. You have to really want to hear what a young person is saying. That takes patience, an open mind, the willingness to see the world from another person's perspective, and the ability to help a kid articulate feelings and thoughts. As you think about becoming a mentor, consider whether you are or want to be this kind of listener.

7. Are You Excited by the Prospect of Helping a Young Person Explore Life's Options?

"Mentoring is a passion," asserts Colonel Anthony Aiken, chairman of the board of directors of the 100 Black Men of Denver. "I mentor because I want kids to know that there are positive options in the world. It's not a personal agenda; it's an agenda for the future.

"I've got an eight-year-old and a twelve-year-old, and I want life to be better for them—for all our kids. I want to help them dare to dream about what's on the other side of the mountain and figure out how they are going to get to that other side. What that boils down to is helping them to not be afraid. And unfortunately, there's lots for kids to be afraid of.

"I have a young boy I am mentoring now, Irving. He is twelve years old. His older brother—sixteen—was just killed in a gang-related incident. What do you say to a kid about that? But you have to say something. He lives with his grandparents, and together we are trying to help Irving understand that he is in charge of his life, that drugs and violence and untimely death are not the certain destiny of young black men, that success and joy and fulfillment are just as much his birthright as anyone else's.

"So what I do is try to show him all the options that he's got available to him. Concrete things. Things that are relevant to his life now. You want to learn to swim, there's the YMCA. You want to get into computers, there's the Denver 100's MOST [Minority Opportunity in Science and Technology] program, a partnership we have with U.S.

West to teach kids about information technology. You want to go to college, there are scholarships and fellowships available to you to pursue just about any academic area you are interested in.

"There are no guarantees in mentoring. The best I can do is open up Irving's horizons, get him to be confident that he can make choices for himself. And I get such a kick out of seeing him mature into those choices. It's like having him grow right in front of my eyes."

Mentoring, at its best, is the process of helping a young person to get excited over learning about the world. Children are by nature curious, but they need to feel safe in order to go exploring. A mentor is a critical part of the safety net that allows a kid to take the risks inherent in dreaming about the future. To play that role, you must be open-minded, patient, and enthusiastic. For a child, every experience, even the most trivial, can be an opportunity to learn. The question you need to ask yourself is whether *you* get charged up about helping a kid learn to learn.

8. Can You Set Clear and Consistent Boundaries?

For a child, a crucial aspect of personal development and learning about the world is understanding and respecting boundaries. This is especially true for young people who come from fractured families and crumbling communities, where they may not have ready access to loving, firm, consistent adult guidance.

You, as a mentor, will be taking on the responsibility of providing such guidance. This does not mean that you will have to be a disciplinarian. You will, however, have to teach your mentee about discipline, about right and wrong, about what is possible and what is not, and about what is appropriate and what is not.

"A kind word and a firm 'no' can mean the difference between life and death in a child's life," explains Andre Howell, director of corporate relations for Allstate Insurance Co., who is a member of the Chicago chapter of the 100. "These are good kids, but it is up to us to give them the encouragement and support to understand how to go after what they want.

"When I see the spark of hope in our kids' eyes, it makes me feel blessed."

Sometimes, mentoring requires tough love. You have to be willing to say no, to correct, to ask hard questions, and to speak unpleasant truths. You might get resistance from the young person you are working with. You might get a sullen look now and then. You might even get a resentful word. But in the long run, what you will get is a whole lot of respect and gratitude.

9. Can You Help a Child Develop Clear and Realistic Expectations?

When you become involved with a child, it is natural to get enthusiastic and to want your relationship to have a profound impact on the young person's life. But part of our job as mentors is to teach youths how to set realistic expectations for themselves. That requires managing your own expectations.

A child who has trouble with basic arithmetic, for instance, will most likely not be able to do complex algebra problems after you have tutored him for a couple of months. Almost certainly, though, he will do much better in arithmetic. And with patience and time, he will probably get to be pretty good in algebra. The important thing is that you do not set up him and yourself for failure by expecting unrealistically rapid progress.

"Patience is the best thing I learned from my mentor," says Wanda, who recently graduated from law school and is in her first year as an attorney with a small firm in San Diego. "Thomas, who was my mentor all through high school, was great at setting small goals on the way to accomplishing big things.

"When we first got matched up by my school, I really wanted to learn computers, but I was terrified of machines. My mind went numb when I even looked at a terminal. So Thomas said, 'Look, don't think about how the thing works or any of that. Let's just start by having you learn how to type a letter.'

"Well, I was good at typing. I figured I could do that. He took me to his office on a Saturday, and we sat down at this fancy-looking machine with a big color monitor. I was terrified. But Thomas just kept talking to me, explaining what he was doing as he turned on the machine and started the word-processing program.

"I typed a letter that Thomas needed to send to one of the suppliers of his plumbing business. When I was done, he showed me how to print on the laser printer and even how to do an envelope. I was so proud. It was a little thing, but I had actually worked on a computer, and I helped my mentor with his work. That was a great feeling.

"That's how it went. Week by week, I would learn something new. Succeed at another task. Before I knew it, I could make my way around word processing, spreadsheets, basic layout and design. It was great. By my sophomore year, I was proficient enough to get a part-time job at a lawyer's office in my neighborhood, doing some basic clerical stuff. That's how I got interested in the law. The two guys I worked for were handling all these interesting civil rights and criminal cases. I would go to the office and just soak all of that stuff up.

"The way I look at it, if Thomas hadn't helped me get over my fear of computers, I would not have gotten that job and probably would not have become a lawyer. And if he had not taught me how to set small, concrete goals and then go about achieving them, I certainly would not have made it through law school. I love telling him that. He gets all embarrassed, but his eyes just shine with how proud he is of what I've accomplished."

10. Are You Prepared to Help a Young Person Define the Individual Meaning of Success?

"I've always been tall," recalls Anthony, who is studying piano at the Mannes School of Music in New York. "Over six feet by the time I was fourteen. So there was a lot of pressure on me to play basketball. I lived in a small town in Indiana—basketball country—and everybody was after me to go out for the team. I happened to be a really good ball player and my parents and teachers kept telling me that a basketball scholarship would be a way to make sure I could go to a good college. And I wasn't that interested. All I wanted to do was play my music, you know.

"When I got a mentor through a youth service organization associated with my church, I was really hoping he would help me figure out how to do what I wanted to do. But at the very first meeting, my mentor started telling me how he could hook me up with a friend of his who was a college coach and that he would start researching scholarships. He just assumed that I would want to play ball, and when I tried to tell him that I wanted to study music, he just shrugged it off. 'No reason you can't do both,' was all he said, like it was up to him to decide.

"I was so disappointed. I needed an ally, and what I got instead was another person who was going to tell me what to do with my life. It was really hard, but I went in and asked my minister for another mentor. I don't know where I got the courage to do that. I guess I wanted help badly enough.

"And help I got. The first thing Khalil, my new mentor, said to me when we met was, 'So I hear you don't want to play basketball. What are you, from another planet?' He had this mischievous grin on his face, and I just cracked up. But then he got all serious, 'You've got a lot of guts, kid. Stick to your guns, and you will be playing your music in Carnegie Hall someday.'

"So, here I am, with a full scholarship—for my creative talents and not my athletic abilities—being involved with something I love and practicing my way to Carnegie Hall."

As a mentor, you see talent, you see potential, you see prospects. It is tempting to act on what you see and to push your mentee toward your vision of success. But remember, your job as a mentor is to help the child you are working with figure out what success means to him or her. That requires that you let go of any preconceived notions of success you may have. For instance, a college degree might seem of paramount importance to you, but may not really be necessary for a kid who wants to be a car mechanic.

The question is whether you are prepared to support a young person in pursuing whatever aspirations he or she has. An open mind and an empathetic heart are essential ingredients of successful mentoring. When you enter a child's life as a mentor, you have to leave your ego at home.

11. Can You Empathize with Young People, Not Sympathize with Them?

"The things I found the most challenging about mentoring," says Robert, a dentist in Cleveland who mentors through Big Brothers/Big Sisters, "are the emotional demands. Honestly, I wasn't really prepared when I first got involved.

"You go into a kid's home, and you see stuff you don't see in your own life. There might be no food in the house. There might be small children that the older ones look after. There might be broken windows and leaking pipes. Whatever it is, your first reaction is to want to fix it. But you can't, so you end up feeling sorry for the kid.

"What you've got to realize, though, is that those are your feelings. There might be broken windows, but there might also be a supportive, loving family. The thing to find out is what the kid is feeling—what's good, what's bad—and then help address those feelings."

A mentor is not a social worker or a savior. A mentor is a guide and an advisor. Therefore, you will have to find the fortitude to resist the urge to solve your mentees' problems or to "rescue" them from the circumstances of their lives. That is hard to do when you become emotionally invested in the life of a child. Yet, to fulfill your proper role as a mentor, you will have to summon the courage to remain an empathetic guide as your mentee deals with problems, makes choices, commits errors, and develops the inner resources necessary to rise above circumstances and turn challenges into opportunities.

12. Are You Prepared to Become an Advocate for a Child?

Although, as we just discussed, a mentor should not think of herself or himself as a rescuer, a mentor must be an *advocate*. There may be situations requiring that you work with your mentee's parents, teachers, or counselors to deal with issues that might be affecting the child's performance in school, or sense of self-worth, or safety.

"My mentee is in the ninth grade," says Kevin L. Patterson, president of the 100 Black Men of Charlotte and member at large of the executive committee of the board of the 100 Black Men of America. "He's a real live wire and can sometimes have a really short fuse. He called me up one day last year and told me that he wanted to beat up this other kid who had been causing trouble. I said, 'Who do you want to be in charge of your life? You or this other kid? Why do you want to give this guy control over what you do? If you get in trouble for fighting at school, it will go on your record, not his. Just cool it and keep your eye on the prize.'

"I then told him how proud I was that he had called

me before taking the situation into his own hands. I said that I realized that it took a lot of self-control to reach out to me, to want to talk things over and not just act out. It made me feel great to help him diffuse the situation. As a mentor, you sometimes have to step in and help smooth the way for the kids."

Do you think you'll feel comfortable taking on the responsibility of advocating on your mentee's behalf? There might be circumstances in the mentee's life that will be uncomfortable for you and situations that may make you uneasy. If this possibility causes you some degree of anxiety, you might want to consider group mentoring before entering into a one-on-one relationship with a young person.

13. Can You "Walk the Walk"?

In Chapter Five, we will deal in depth with the challenges, surprises, and joys of serving as a role model to a young person. But for the moment, you should ask yourself whether you are prepared to take an honest look at the way you act, speak, carry yourself—at the kind of example you provide a child.

"I remember driving on the beltway with my mentee, Carlos," says Sylvia, a systems specialist with a Federal agency in Washington, who mentors through a program at the YMCA. "This guy in a Porsche cut right in front of me. But I mean close. I hit the brake and cursed him out.

"Carlos, he was about eight then, giggled. And suddenly, I felt so embarrassed. I was supposed to be setting a good example for this kid, and here I was cussing and carrying on.

"It really made me think about what it means to put

yourself forward as a role model. You can't just tell kids 'do this' and 'don't do that.' You have to show them how to live by those rules."

Kids look up to adults in ways we can never imagine. Our words have serious impact on them and our actions affect them deeply—whether we are aware of it or not. The mentoring relationship holds us to the standard we expect from our young people and demands that we not only *say* but also *do* what we consider to be the right thing.

14. Are You Prepared for the Necessity of Ending a Mentoring Relationship?

The end of a mentoring relationship is often its most important stage. It is an acknowledgment that the young person has come far enough to be independent. The distance that the separation creates allows the youth to incorporate the mentor's best qualities, to gain more self-assurance, and to define more clearly the personal boundaries. In short, the end of a mentoring relationship is an important rite of passage.

"It was so hard to let go of Melody when she graduated from high school," remembers Sarah, a secretary with a financial investment firm in New York, who mentors through her company's corporate program. "We had been together for three years, and I'd seen her through a lot of really positive changes. Melody developed greater confidence and self-esteem during the time we were together. She received her high school degree—a childhood dream—and was working at an administrative job in a bank. But it wasn't as if her life was perfect. She still had to commute to her job on Wall Street from her apartment in a crack tenement building in East Harlem. She still had to take care of her schizophrenic mother and supervise her younger sister. Her boyfriend was pressuring her to have a baby and she told me that they were no longer using condoms during sex.

"I was so worried that Melody would slip through the cracks if I wasn't there to give her support. Then, out of the blue, she stopped calling me and wouldn't return any of my messages. She didn't want to see me anymore, plain and simple. I guess when it's time, it's time, but I was devastated. I just had to hope that she had the strength—and resources—to make it on her own, without me looking out for her. At that point, all I could go on was my faith in who she was.

"We've been out of touch for two years now. There isn't a week I don't think about her. I know, though, that our paths will cross again. I know that she'll take care of herself. I believe that what I've taught her and exposed her to has made a lasting impression, a kind of imprint. My last message to her was that no matter what happens, or has happened, she is always welcome in my life.

"Melody knows in her heart that I genuinely cared for her and always will. This gets me through whenever I imagine what she is facing as a young woman in today's complex world. I have to believe that I have influenced her as deeply as she has affected me."

When a mentor is overly attached, it is especially difficult for a young person to move on. Ask yourself whether you are willing to take on the emotional challenge of getting involved with a child and then, when it is time, letting go.

Some hard questions were asked in this chapter. The purpose was to help you think through your commitment to mentoring. I hope that after having done so you are even more excited by the prospect of giving your time to a child. In the coming chapters, the practical details of role modeling, the stages of a mentoring relationship, and the practices of successful mentors will be further explored.

What You Can Do:

1. Ask yourself what you want to get out of mentoring.
2. Consider what you have to offer a child.
3. Decide what you would like to accomplish through mentoring.

CHAPTER THREE

Doing It Right: The Ten Tickets to Mentoring

There are no wrong notes.

—THELONIOUS MONK

Mentoring a young person is very much like playing jazz. The melody is the sum total of your life's experience and the ways in which you communicate it to your mentee are the riffs—the improvised variations of the moment. No one riff is like another, and all of our melodies are unique.

There are, in fact, no wrong notes in mentoring. But just as you need to master the fundamentals of music in order to express yourself fully, in order to be an effective mentor you should work to understand the basic attitudes and skills necessary to reach a young person and to make a difference in his or her life.

In 1998, the 100 Black Men of America asked the Gallup Organization to conduct a research study of our mentoring program in order to determine which components were the most successful in reaching young people. Our purpose was to incorporate the experiences, impressions, and suggestions of our practicing mentors into a structured training program for future mentors. Interviews were held with more than eight hundred of our mentors from chapters throughout the country.

The Gallup Organization focused on four areas of concern in the mentoring relationship:

1. The most important attitudes and behaviors for mentors to practice.
2. The most productive behaviors for developing an effective relationship with a mentee.
3. The special characteristics of especially effective mentors.
4. The defining themes of a mentoring relationship.

The mentors included men ranging in age from their twenties to their sixties, with a median age of 48. Their education level spanned the gamut—from less than high school diplomas to postgraduate degrees, with 98 percent of the participants having at least some postsecondary education. The income level of the mentors in the study was also quite high, with 77 percent reporting annual household incomes above $55,000. For additional background information, several focus groups were also held with young people who were being mentored in programs sponsored by the 100.

The results of the study were clear and concise: Ten key skills and behaviors were identified as essential for productive mentoring and for deriving full satisfaction from the mentoring relationship. We call them the "Ten Tickets to Mentoring":

ONE: Believing that mentoring is building a relationship

TWO: Acting as a role model for your mentee

THREE: Talking to your mentee about what is right and wrong

FOUR: Projecting wholesome values to your mentee

FIVE: Taking satisfaction from mentoring because you believe that you have something important to offer to the right young person

SIX: Doing everything you can to develop trust with your mentee

SEVEN: Telling your mentee that you care about him or her

EIGHT: Pointing out the right behavior for certain situations

NINE: Helping your mentee develop goals

TEN: Listening to whatever your mentee wants to talk about.

The "Ten Tickets to Mentoring" should be used as a starting point in the mentoring relationship. The "Tickets" are a foundation of fundamentals upon which each of us can build our own improvisations in helping young people to realize their dreams and to explore and discover options they might not have known existed.

TICKET #1: *Believe that Mentoring Is Building a Relationship*

"To be a mentor," explains William Hammond, president of the 100 Black Men of Sonoma County and member of the National Board of Directors of the 100, "is to make a positive commitment to a relationship. You might be able to be a role model by being successful at what you do or by carrying yourself a certain way, but when you agree to be a mentor, you agree to be there for a young person.

"As a mentor, *you show up no matter what.* And there might be hard times, times when the young man or woman challenges you or needs more of your time. But that's like any relationship. The point is you can't look at mentoring as just a project you give a couple of hours a week to, you have to be prepared to make the emotional investment necessary to build trust, to win respect, to have an impact."

Think about what it is that you hope to accomplish as a mentor. Most likely, you want to help a young person face the difficulties of adolescence or succeed in school or reach for a dream—or all of the above. Tutoring, inspiring, challenging, and providing opportunities are not enough. You must enter into a child's life, develop trust, earn confidence, find common ground. For, in truth, mentoring can only begin after you and your mentee come to regard one another as important people in each other's lives.

"At first, the relationship challenged me in ways that I had not expected," recalls Steve, an internet entrepreneur who mentors through a corporate-sponsored program in New York. "It was like hitting a brick wall. Tanya was pretty uncommunicative in those early days. I'd call and would rarely get a call back. We would go places, and I would do most of the talking, occasionally getting a monosyllabic response. Sometimes it got outright frustrating.

"But I said, 'Wait a minute. Who is the adult here? Look at what this kid has had to deal with.' Her dad left the family when Tanya was eight, right after her little brother was born. Her mother worked the night shift, and Tanya often had to look after her brother. It's not like she had any reason to trust or rely on adults. And here I was getting ticked off because she wasn't returning my phone calls.

"Tanya wasn't about to risk reaching out to me, this guy she didn't know. She had internalized so much rejection, she did everything possible to avoid it. She simply did not have the social skills at that point to be fifty percent of the relationship. Once I understood and accepted that, I felt all right about taking on much more of the responsibility for making contact and keeping the relationship going.

"It took almost a year, but she finally started to open up. I'll never forget the first time she called me on her own. She had gotten a small part in a play that she had auditioned for, and she called to tell me the news. I can't tell you what it felt like to know that I'd made enough of a difference for her to want to share this success with me. I couldn't have been happier if I'd won the lottery."

You and the young person you mentor will need time

to get to know each other, to develop mutual expectations for the relationship, to learn what works best for the two of you. To make sure you have that time, you will need to be patient and persistent. Only if you believe you are building something valuable, that you are building an important relationship, will you be able to create a bond that will allow you to have a lasting impact on your mentee's life.

TICKET #2: *Act as a Role Model for Your Mentee*

One of the key concepts in "Mentoring the 100 Way" is that young people learn by modeling themselves on the adults in their lives. As a mentor, you will be one of the most important adults for your mentee, and as such you will carry a special responsibility to model positive attitudes and behaviors.

"There is a difference between celebrities and role models," states Ron Williams, former director of diversity for Nike and member of the 100 Black Men of America. "We can't all be Michael Jordan, but we can be teachers, pastors, mentors, friends."

Our children have too many distant heroes and not enough intimate role models. Many kids spend more time watching their favorite actors and athletes and listening to their favorite musicians than they do talking or doing things with the adults in their lives. No wonder that so many of them pattern themselves on these remote but exciting stars and aspire to be ball players, models, or rappers.

The problem is especially acute for African American youth. Many simply do not get to see black doctors, business people, lawyers, pilots, and scientists.

"Too often, the media present black males in a negative

light," asserts Bill Campbell, mayor of Atlanta, who is one of the founding members of that city's chapter of the 100 Black Men of America. "African American men are portrayed as drug dealers, as criminals, as con artists. They do not show black men in positions of accomplishment and authority.

"We cannot forget our roots and our tradition of bringing others along. That is why I speak at every school that invites me, so the young people will see that there is someone in the public eye whom they can identify with and who cares about them. African American youth are proud to see successful black men, and it is our obligation to serve as role models for them."

All children, regardless of their ethnic or socioeconomic background, need positive role models. And as a mentor, you will be in a position to provide your mentee with a model for how to learn, how to treat other people, how to approach problems, how to express oneself—in short, how to lead one's life. This is a heavy (but doable) responsibility, and it is crucial that you understand what it takes to be a role model. Chapter Four, "What They See Is What They'll Be," examines in detail this vital aspect of the mentoring relationship.

TICKET #3: *Talk to Your Mentee About What Is Right and Wrong*

When I think back to my childhood, one of the things I remember most clearly and am especially thankful for is the strong sense of values we had in our community. It was not just our parents who taught us right from wrong, it was the responsibility of all the adults—especially the elders—to guide us on the correct path. If you stepped out of line anywhere in town, you would first get reprimanded by the neighbors, and then you would get it from your parents. It sounds tough, but such discipline was done out of tenderness and caring, out of a desire to give us kids the moral skills we would need to make our way in the world.

The desire to lead and inspire young people is still present in our community, but the way of life—the "village"—that facilitated the teaching of values is gone for the most part. Here again, formal mentoring must take the place of the informal social interactions between youth and adults that were so common back in the fifties and sixties when I was growing up. We as mentors must now take the place of our elders and talk with young people about what is right and wrong.

"The way I think about it," explains U.S. Army Colonel Anthony Aiken, chairman of the board of the Denver chapter of the 100 Black Men of America, "you can affect lives by simply helping kids avoid the mistakes that you made. That's real practical mentoring. And it's easy to explain.

"Say you've got a kid who has a tendency to make trouble at school. All you've got to say is: 'I got into fights at school until I got kicked out. It took me a year to catch up, and it cost me a spot on the basketball team.' Now, I'm not saying make it up, but we all have real-life experiences that we learned our lessons from, so it's a matter of communicating those lessons to the kids. You just have to be creative.

"The kids get it. It's real concrete for them when you talk from your own experience. They understand that you learned the hard way and that you are trying to make the going a little easier for them. They might not always show it, but they do appreciate it. And they do learn.

"The bottom line is that I want our young people to be better than I am. So I figure it's my job to share with them as much as I've learned."

TICKET #4: *Project Wholesome Values*

Talking with kids about right and wrong is only part of the responsibility of a mentor, however. To have a real impact, you have to show your mentee that you live by the values you teach. Young people are really sensitive to inconsistency and hypocrisy. So if you practice the "Do as I say, not as I do" philosophy, they are not likely to have much respect for you or for what you are trying to teach them.

This does not mean that you have to be saintly to be a mentor. You just have to be honest and thoughtful. If you want to teach the young girl you are mentoring to treat her elders with respect, make sure that you show her that you are respectful to the elders in your own life. If you want to instill in your mentee that it is important to honor his commitments, set an example by honoring yours. Remember, as a mentor you are first and foremost a role model.

Bruce Harper, who as a New York Jets running back and punt returner from 1977 to 1985 was selected Most Valuable Player, recalls, "When I was playing in the National Football League, we would go into schools to talk to the kids. It was always a moving experience, but there was this one time that really stands out for me.

"I was talking with a group of about twenty or thirty kids. They were all asking questions, getting all excited. But there was this one guy who just kept looking me up and down, kind of shaking his head. Finally, he said, 'Yeah, I am going to play football, so I get some nice clothes like that.'

"That really brought me up short, you know. I hesitated and said, 'The most important thing is that you do what you love. Not for the money, but for the passion.' And I meant that. I loved football more than anything else. But what kind of message was I really sending? Did the expensive clothes take away from what I was trying to communicate? I thought a lot about that since, and it has really informed the way I approach kids. Just saying something isn't enough, it's the total package that counts."

TICKET #5: *Take Satisfaction from Mentoring Because You Believe That You Have Something Important to Offer to the Right Young Person*

"When you first start mentoring, it's a bit like having your first kid," says Randy Walker, chair of the mentoring committee of the 100 Black Men of Metropolitan Detroit. "You wonder if you are going to be able to handle it, if you have what it takes to help a child grow and develop. But that only lasts until the first time you see your mentee tackle a problem you've helped him deal with or say something that sounds a lot like something you might say. That's when a real sense of satisfaction replaces the doubts. That's when you get the affirmation that you do have something special to offer.

"I have a passion for mentoring, for making a difference in a child's life. I know that I bring that to every relationship, but still, with every young person I mentor I wonder if I will be able to reach him or her. With my current mentee, it took a while. He did not trust me at first. As a matter of fact, he was wary of most adults. So, it was a struggle just to connect.

"But we've stuck with it, and I can see how he has really matured over the two years we've been together. I can see it in his attitude. He reaches out to me and tells me how much he appreciates my time. That's a great feeling.

"Mentoring is about consistency and repetition. Sooner or later, you see that what you are saying and doing is having an impact. You share with the kids, and in the process, you learn, too. You learn with them and from them. And they keep you young. The reward and the joy of mentoring comes from the inside, through genuine self-fulfillment."

You may not know before you start mentoring what that special quality is that you have to offer a young person. But if your instincts tell you that you want to share your experiences and your compassion with a child, trust your heart and follow its call. As you take that leap of faith and reach out to a young person, you will learn about the gifts you possess and experience the satisfaction of touching a young life.

TICKET #6: *Do Everything You Can to Develop Mutual Trust with Your Mentee*

"The trust of my mentors is something I have always cherished," says Johnny E. Parham, Jr., former executive director of the Thurgood Marshall Scholarship Fund. "When these men whom I looked up to—whom I trusted—said 'We believe in you,' I felt so proud, so supported. It helped me have confidence in myself and my choices. It helped me take risks and stand up for the things I believed in. And it helped me to live with integrity, in a way that would make my mentors proud.

"Two of the men who had the greatest influence on my life were Whitney Young and Benjamin Mays. Dr. Mays was the president of Morehouse College when I was a student there, and he was like a god to everyone on campus. He despised segregation and instilled in each and every student the pride of being African American. Dr. Mays would speak in front of the student body every Tuesday in the chapel, and if any of us had questions, he would invite us to come by his office for further discussion. He reached out and showed interest in us and our futures.

"Whitney Young was the dean of the School of Social Work at Atlanta University when I was there in 1960; he then went on to become the executive director of the National Urban League. Whitney became a mentor to me while I was a student and continued to be for a long time after.

"I was also very much influenced by the philosophy of Dr. Martin Luther King, Jr., and was really steeped in nonviolent civil action. I belonged to the Appeal for Human Rights in Atlanta. In the spring of 1960, we planned a massive assault for civil rights by setting up simultaneous sit-ins on several campuses throughout the city. We were serious about eliminating segregation and were literally prepared to die for our cause.

"As our group was organizing, we turned to Dr. Mays and Whitney Young for counsel. There was never a question among any of us that they would not support our plans. We knew that they would not discourage us because they believed in us. We were confident of their trust.

"And indeed, they heard us out and then helped us

think through the potential consequences of what we were going to do. They let us know that they cared about us and our cause. They were true mentors."

Mentoring is a relationship based on trust. Building that trust between you and the young person you are mentoring is an essential step in developing a lasting and productive relationship. The important point to remember about trust, however, is that it cuts two ways. You have to win your mentee's trust in order for him or her to open up to you. And, in turn, you must learn to trust your mentee and demonstrate that trust time and time again during the relationship.

Showing up and following through are sure ways to begin to build trust. You can also assure the young person you are mentoring that what you talk about remains between the two of you. As you begin to establish a bond, show that you trust your mentee. A good first step is to give the young person your home telephone number. In doing so, you will show that you value the relationship and trust the youth to respect your boundaries. You can then continue to forge a trusting relationship by asking him or her to help you with an important task or accompanying you on a family outing.

Exactly how you go about building trust is going to depend on you and your mentee. The important thing to remember is that this is probably the most crucial aspect of mentoring. You need to devote careful thought and attention to establishing a relationship in which you and your mentee will have genuine faith in each other.

TICKET #7: *Tell Your Mentee That You Care About Him or Her*

When I was a kid, I would walk into a grocery store or the barber shop and there would be a couple of adults from the neighborhood who would start commenting on how quickly I was growing or what a good young man I was turning out to be. It was kind of embarrassing to be the center of attention, but it sure felt good to know that all these people cared about me and noticed my presence. As a mentor, you have a similar opportunity to give young people that same good feeling by letting them know how much you care about them.

"We are overwhelmed by reports about our kids becoming alienated," says Tupac Hunter, member of the Metropolitan Detroit chapter of the 100. "Kids feel that no one cares, so they become numb. All it takes to make a difference is one important person in their lives who makes them feel that they're special—someone to encourage, uplift, give positive feedback.

"I was raised in a lower-middle-class community in Detroit and had the benefit of growing up safe. I was lucky to have folks who spent time with me and who paid attention to my needs. I knew these people loved me. And knowing people love you makes you love yourself. So when I faced setbacks, I did not fall apart or turn in on myself.

"I know how important it was for me to have that caring and love in my life. I want our kids to know how good it feels to be loved and to learn to love themselves."

It is difficult for many of us to express our emotions. But it is not necessary to expose your soul, or deliver long speeches, or make grand gestures to let a young person know that you care. It's as simple as telling your mentee how proud you are of her. How you enjoy spending time with her. How pleased you are that you've had a chance to get to know her.

"A young man in our 'Rites of Passage' program once asked me why I was giving up my Saturdays to be there with him," recounts Omotolokun Omokunde, president of the 100 Black Men of Milwaukee. "I looked him straight in the eye and said, 'Because you are special.' And I meant it. Well, the expression on his face was worth a decade of Saturdays to me. It was a real spiritual high."

TICKET #8: *Point Out the Right Behavior for Certain Situations*

"My mentor, Tracy, and I didn't even know each other for very long when I got into some heavy stuff at school," says Vickie, now studying accounting at a community college in Los Angeles. She was mentored through a program that brought entertainment executives into local public schools. "I was in eleventh grade, and there was this posse of girls who always made trouble for me and my girlfriend Shawna. We'd had a few fights in the halls, but mostly it was just trash talking.

"Things got bad, though, when one of the other girls went after Shawna's boyfriend. Shawna just lost control. She started acting all crazy, saying she was going to cut the girl. And I got really scared.

"What was I supposed to do? I couldn't just let it happen, but I also didn't know how to stop it. Worst of all, it felt like there was no one I could talk to.

"When I saw Shawna put a razor in her locker, I knew

I had to get some help. And the only person I could think of was Tracy. I don't know why, but somehow I knew that she wouldn't judge me and she would know what to do.

"I called her up and presented the situation in really vague terms. Like, 'What would you do if you knew that someone was going to do something really bad?' She listened to me for a while and then cut right to it. 'Vickie, if you know there is going to be trouble, you've got to let someone at school know.'

"I said that would be ratting out a friend. 'Yes,' she answered, 'but you are probably going to prevent her from really messing up her life.' We talked about it for a long time, weighing all the different possibilities. And what I really appreciated about the way Tracy talked to me was that she was really sure about what she believed was right, but she also didn't brush off what I was feeling. It was sort of like a negotiation, where we were both listening to each other and trying to come up with a course of action that would feel right for both of us.

"Finally, we agreed that I would let Shawna know that I thought it was crazy to get violent over a guy—over anything or anybody, for that matter. I would tell her that I spoke to Tracy about the situation and, if I had to, I was going to talk to the school counselor about it.

"I was scared to death when it came time to actually confront Shawna. I had never done anything like that in my life. She was really mad, too. For about a week. Then she came up to me in the hall and said, 'He isn't worth it, is he?' And we just laughed, girlfriend like. 'No, nobody's worth that,' I said.

"Things were never the same between Shawna and me, but I knew that I had done the right thing. And my relationship with Tracy really changed after that. I knew I could count on her to help me find my footing, no matter how hard the situation. It's a great feeling to have someone like that."

There will be situations—some trivial, others serious—in which you will have to guide your mentee toward the right way to act. It is very important that in such cases you pay careful attention to where the young person is coming from. What are the concerns? What are the cultural norms at play? What values? To be effective, you will have to be better at listening than at giving advice. And always remember, if there is danger of physical harm to your mentee or any other person, it is appropriate for you to take direct and immediate action by informing your sponsoring mentoring program or by going directly to a family member or to school or law-enforcement authorities. If you feel that the situation calls for such measures, always explain to your mentee what you are going to do and why.

TICKET #9: *Help Your Mentee Develop Goals*

Kids are by nature dreamers. They fantasize about going to the moon, or finding a hidden treasure, or winning gold medals at the Olympics, or starring in their favorite television show. They dream about smaller things, too, like getting a pair of in-line skates, or doing better in social studies, or learning how to draw, or going to an amusement park. As a mentor, you have a wonderful opportunity to encourage these dreams and to teach your mentees how to set attainable goals on the way to realizing their dreams.

"When I was growing up in White Oaks, Texas," says

Byron Hunt, who played pro football for the New York Giants and the Detroit Lions, "there were three big things in our town—religion, community, and sports. And sports seemed out of the question for me since I was the kind of kid who was always picked last for any team, even when it was my brothers who were choosing sides. For the most part, I stayed in the yard and practiced basketball with my little sister.

"But then I met Tommy Atkins. He coached track and football at our school and trained me to excel in both. It was Tommy who encouraged me to go out for track, which turned out to be the best thing I ever did. I didn't know how fast I was until I tried, but then I knew that I had a special skill. Tommy kept encouraging me, pushing me to see how much I had in me. Every day, it would be, 'Let's see if we can shave a few more seconds off that time.'

"Thanks to Tommy, I became a fast runner, and that really helped my career. I got a scholarship for football and basketball at SMU in Dallas and signed with the Giants in 1981. I am a big man—I was a linebacker—but I could run as fast as some of those little guys. That was my secret weapon.

"The greatest thing about Tommy was that he instilled in us the idea that whatever you do, do your best. Work hard, make small improvements, until you are at the top of your game. He believed in us and demanded that we respect ourselves. Those are lessons that have served me well throughout my life."

Knowing how to set realistic, attainable goals is a skill, but it is also a state of mind. You have to have enough confidence in yourself to know that you can reach the goal you set in order to take the risk of trying for it. And every accomplished objective, in turn, increases your faith in yourself and makes it easier to reach for bigger prizes.

It is important to keep this in mind as you go about encouraging your mentee to set goals. Find out what the young person dreams about, and then discuss how you can break down the dream into several smaller objectives that build on each other. For example, if your mentee wants to be a veterinarian, you can suggest volunteering as a dog walker at a shelter or kennel, help her research the educational qualifications necessary to be accepted into a veterinary college, maybe even try to get her a part-time job in a local vet's office. The process of working toward a major goal will help her to develop an essential life skill and a few successes will help boost her confidence as she makes plans and prepares for her future.

TICKET #10: *Listen to Whatever Your Mentee Wants to Talk About*

"I had a boy I mentored a couple of years back who really taught me something about what young people are looking for," says Dennis, who mentors through a Boston program that is organized by his union. "I met Patrick when he was in eleventh grade. He was an honor student and his high school résumé looked like a college résumé. He had traveled all over the country with his parents and seemed the most unlikely candidate for someone who needed a mentor. I kept looking at him and thinking, 'Why would such an accomplished and seemingly secure young man sign up for the mentor program? What does he really need?'

"It became apparent early on in our relationship that

what he was looking for was a relationship with an adult who could be objective and had no special agenda. His mother had recently remarried and he was having a difficult time adjusting to his new stepfather. He felt disloyal discussing this with his mom and I represented a concerned older person who would listen to him without a preconceived set of expectations.

"I had to keep reminding myself that this was a seventeen-year-old kid. He might be a strong person, but we all need people to talk to. So I stayed with the simple things, just conversation, you know. And that is when we began to click. He opened up to me and included me in his hopes and dreams and fears. Through our conversations, I also found myself exploring parts of myself that I hadn't thought about for years.

"I particularly remember driving to the picnic celebrating the end of the mentoring program for the school year. Patrick talked nonstop for thirty-five minutes on the way there and for thirty-five minutes on the way back. He talked about going off to college, about wanting to be independent, about his fears of being homesick while away. He talked about his girlfriend, his frustrations with the Red Sox. And I encouraged him to enjoy himself, to expand his horizons, to find his vision for life, to dream.

"That turned into one of the best relationships with a mentee that I've had. All Patrick needed was somebody to talk to. I was lucky to be that person."

Being a good listener affirms for your mentees that their concerns—no matter how trivial they may seem—are important, this ticket being an *essential* responsibility of a mentor. The best way to show young people that you care about them is to listen to them, engage their feelings, and help them learn to listen to themselves.

As you begin to mentor, use the "Ten Tickets to Mentoring" as a way to check your effectiveness and progress with the young people in your life. Each relationship is special and has its own dynamics. Therefore, some of the skills and attitudes we have discussed in this chapter may be more important than others with one young person, and a slightly different set may be needed for someone else.

These "Ten Tickets to Mentoring" are the foundation of the 100's successful Miracles of Mentoring program. They're working for us and I trust that they will work for you.

What You Can Do:

1. Learn about the techniques of mentoring.
2. Talk to men and women who are currently mentoring.
3. Join a program that provides guidance and training for young people.

CHAPTER FOUR

What They See Is What They'll Be: Mentors, Role Models, and Celebrities

A stream cannot rise higher than its source.

—ANNA J COOPER

Before you enter the life of a child as a mentor, consider what your main purpose in life is. Children learn by observing and imitating everyone around them: siblings, parents, aunts, uncles, grandparents, people in the neighborhood, teachers, coaches, cartoon characters, actors, musicians, ball players—the list goes on and on. Young people take on the attitudes, behaviors, and beliefs that surround them. That is how they make sense of the world and search out their place in it.

This thirst for knowledge is not simply curiosity, it is a survival mechanism. Ironically, it also poses serious danger to kids' survival if there is not sufficient caring and thoughtful guidance in their lives. Just as babies will happily reach for a sharp knife or an electrical outlet if left unattended, children will pattern themselves after whatever role models are available to them.

"I am the seventh of eight kids," explains Robert McDonald, who is prelaw at Morehouse College, and who was mentored by Lee Bush, Sr., of the Jackson, Mississippi, chapter of the 100 Black Men of America. "It was just my mom and us kids—five brothers and two sisters. No one in the family graduated high school. No one went to college. All I knew, from the time I was in grade school, was hanging out with my brothers. We all belonged to the 'Nine O'clock Posse,' which was basically a gang of drug dealers.

"That's how I learned. I got praised if I beat somebody up. And I got beat up if I stepped out of line. By the time I started middle school, when I was thirteen, I was one tough character.

"Lucky for me, the 100 was working with my school. Suddenly, there was another group of black men that I saw regularly, and they talked about things like education, careers, giving back. I looked at the way they carried themselves, the way they spoke, the clothes they wore, and I said, 'Wait a minute, maybe there's another way to be cool.'

"So, I started paying attention. It was like the world opened up for me. I got to see so many different people doing so many different things. And I started getting praised for things like avoiding a fight, doing my homework, helping out on a field trip, doing well on a test—the right things.

"It felt so good. It wasn't just the sense of accomplishment and possibility, but the knowledge that there were so many adults out there who really cared about what happened to me. I wanted to do well to make them proud. And I did. I was the first in my family to graduate from high school—there is now another graduate—and the first to go to college.

"That's a great responsibility. When I go back home, I always stop by my old high school and tell the kids what I am doing in college. I know what having positive role models did for me, so I reach out and tell my story. I want them to say, 'Hey, if Robert can do it, I can do it.' "

Robert's experience illustrates the challenges our young people face today and the critical role mentors play in helping them choose a path toward success.

In October of 1997, the members of the 100 Black Men of Louisville, Kentucky, gathered together with 30 young African American men from local middle and high schools. In front of an audience of parents, supporters, and former mentees, they launched "Project MALE" (Men Advancing Leadership Effectiveness), a mentoring program designed to provide youth from at-risk environments with positive after-school experiences.

"We started out with the idea of giving the young people something to do each day after they get out of school," explains Lamont Collins, president of the Louisville chapter. "That idle time between school and when the parents get home is when a lot of kids get into trouble. We wanted to put them in situations where they would see positive African American male adult role models and would also be in a positive peer environment.

"Ours is a holistic, full-circle mentoring program. We hired a full-time program director who created a really flexible structure for mentors and organized a wide range of activities for the kids that includes tutoring, career shadowing, paid internships, retreats, volunteerism, camping, travel, and scholarship opportunities."

Lamont Collins clearly remembers that first day of "Project MALE." Each of the young men in the program received a hug, a handshake, and a pledge from the members of the 100 Black Men of Louisville that they would receive support and guidance in creating a future for themselves and their community.

Now in its fourth year, "Project MALE" has grown to include 100 young men from Louisville's most challenged schools. The program, which connects sixth to twelfth graders with members of the 100, focuses on four areas of youth development:

1. *Education:* Mentors work with participants to help them successfully complete high school and to explore and attend postsecondary or vocational institutions.
2. *Career and entrepreneurship:* Mentors help the young men to explore a variety of careers and facilitate, create, and promote economic and entrepreneurial opportunities.
3. *Family and heritage:* Mentors help their mentees become more aware of their heritage and family responsibilities, both current and future. Special emphasis is placed on challenging young men to fulfill these responsibilities.

4. *Community and leadership:* Mentors involve the participants in building coalitions and participating in community activities with youth ministries and other culturally diverse youth groups with common interests.

The list of the program activities is truly impressive:

- one-to-one and group mentoring
- weekly after-school and weekend group sessions
- tutoring in math, science, reading, and social studies
- college and scholarship support
- goal-setting workshops
- family-centered activities
- parent support group activities
- early fatherhood prevention and support
- African American heritage activities
- community service and leadership training
- youth forums and social activities with other youth groups
- creation of youth-run businesses
- career exploration and workplace tours
- support in finding employment
- shadowing and interning with mentors
- job skills and employment workshops
- American Economic System and Stock Market Game
- elementary school read-ins.

"Project MALE" operates in cooperation with the Jefferson County Public School System, which identifies mentees and even provides office space for the program. The 100 Black Men of Louisville also enlists a variety of other partners in this project.

"Recently we ran a really exciting program for kids sixteen or older who were in gangs or thinking of joining," explains Lamont Collins. "Together with Habitat for Humanity and the Rotary Club of Louisville, we built a house in a low-income neighborhood.

"We had our young guys working side by side with work-release inmates from the Department of Corrections and adult volunteers. We had these low-risk inmates—under supervision yet being informally mentored by our members—telling at-risk teenagers what could happen to them and showing them the consequences of their actions. During the project, the Jefferson County 4-H ran violence prevention workshops for the youth. And everyone learned vocational and social skills in the process."

Jeffrey L. Berry is program director of the Louisville chapter. "We are always looking for creative ways to mentor through partnerships," he says. "Our entrepreneurship program, 'T-Shirts & Stuff,' is a good example. It is a youth business that we started with less than $2,500 to make customized T-shirts and such. Now, through our work with the Jefferson County Health Department, the Organization of Black Airline Pilots, the University of Louisville, and others, the program has grown into a digital technology business. The kids are making photo buttons, business cards, the whole gamut. And we are doing tutoring on computers that have multimedia encyclopedias and Internet access. That kind of growth is only possible when you have the whole community involved."

"I'm a product of my environment—I was raised in Detroit in the early 1970s," attests William Hammond of Sonoma County. "My community had doctors, postmen, bus drivers, teachers. Everyone I came in contact with became my role model, and I didn't look at any occupation as one I could not aspire to. I didn't know there were any limitations to what I could be and I was confident in my career choices.

"When I moved to California for high school, there were few African Americans. So I decided to attend a historically black college, Houston-Tillotson College in Austin, Texas. That was the most nurturing place I ever encountered as an adult."

Supportive situations, intact communities, nourishing environments all provide easy access to a variety of adult role models. Yet, nowadays, young people spend a lot more time with other kids and with the images of the celebrities they idolize than they do with their parents, members of their extended families, neighbors, or community and spiritual leaders. In this environment, the important distinction between mentors, role models, and heroes is lost, and children are left to pattern their behavior on that of other children and of star athletes, rappers and rockers, and Hollywood personalities.

At best, what this leads to is that our children all want to be "like Mike." The problem, of course, as television personality Tavis Smiley points out is that "they will never *be* Michael Jordan. The fact is, a black child has a one in eight thousand chance of becoming a player in the NBA; and one chance in ten thousand of playing baseball in the major leagues."

Given such odds, it is not surprising that so many kids lose hope. With no models for attainable dreams and little guidance in building their futures, children have a hard time seeing that a world of options is available to them. It is up to us as mentors to help them see the potential within themselves and to understand that they can achieve anything they set their minds and hearts on.

It is said that "life is the first gift, love is the second, and understanding is the third." When you give love and understanding to a child, you create a legacy of hope, inner strength, and compassion that will grow and multiply through generations.

Mentors, Role Models, and Celebrities

"The battles that count aren't the ones for gold medals," Olympian gold medal hero Jesse Owens said. "The struggles within yourself—the invisible, inevitable battles inside all of us—that's where it's all at."

As much as we might understand this, it seems part of human nature to look to those among us who achieve the extraordinary—the celebrities—as our ideals. In some measure, we all want to be "like Mike," or Spike, or Lauryn, or Oprah, or Malcolm. Kids, particularly, tend to idolize these larger-than-life people and want to emulate them.

Our celebrities themselves, however, are the first to tell us that we should not confuse them with role models. Charles Barkley puts it this way: "I am not a role model . . . I am paid to wreak havoc on the basketball court. Parents should be role models. Just because I dunk a basketball doesn't mean I should raise your kids."

In his inimitable way, "Sir" Charles makes clear that his ability with a basketball does not make him a positive example for children. This point is reinforced by Hank Aaron, one of the early members of the 100 Black Men of America, who stresses that there can be real danger in young people looking up to celebrities with whom they have no personal contact.

"There used to be these commercials on television, in which a famous football player was shown using snuff tobacco," Hank recalls. "Through my work with college athletes, I met this kid who was a great football player. He really looked up to this guy on the television. Idolized him. So he started using snuff.

"When he graduated, he was recruited by a pro team. During his physical during training camp, the doctors discovered bubbles on his lip and gums. They turned out to be cancer, and this young man died within a year. It still makes me sad to think about such a terrible waste of a young life.

"A lot of guys don't understand that there are kids out there following every move they make. And listening to every word they say. I was an athlete for twenty-three years, and let me tell you, when you are out there playing, you are so focused, it's hard to think about anything else. But I always tried to remind myself that whatever I did—on or off the field—would have an influence on the people who watched me play and had faith in my ability. This is a great responsibility for all of us in the public eye."

The trouble with celebrities is that all we see of them are isolated snippets—moments of greatness, of weakness, of triumph, of defeat. We do not get to see up close how they deal with the daily inner struggles that Jesse Owens talked about.

We can turn to the very roots of mentoring to understand the distinction between a celebrity, a mentor, and a role model. Remember that the word *mentor* comes from the name of Odysseus' friend, Mentor, to whom, in Homer's epic, the hero entrusted the care and guidance of his son before setting off on his great voyage. "Many they were whose cities he saw, whose minds he learned of," but wise Odysseus knew that a child needs the constant presence and loving counsel of an adult in order to grow.

A hero, then, is someone whose achievements we admire and who inspires us to greatness. A role model is someone who we admire as a person and whose behavior, attitudes, and beliefs we emulate. A mentor is someone who not only serves as a role model but also takes an active part in helping us grow into the kinds of people we want to be.

As a mentor, you need to work to help your mentees understand this distinction. The idea is not to get kids to stop admiring their celebrities but to be realistic and discriminating about what they can learn from them. For instance, if your mentee idolizes Dennis Rodman and is thinking of getting a tattoo on his forearm, you can encourage him to consider how that decision might affect his future.

You also have to help your mentees recognize that there are scores of role models within easy reach, if they know how to look for them. The important thing is to spark young peoples' imaginations, to show them that there are ordinary folk out there doing extraordinary things. The Aviation Camp at the Louisville chapter of the 100 is a great example of this.

"Pilots are good role models, because we are high

achievers and yet spiritually grounded," explains Houston Mills, a former marine fighter pilot who now flies Boeing 727 jets for UPS and is the director of the Aviation Camp. "It's an easy sell with kids. We bring in members of the Organization of Black Airline Pilots, and you should see the surprise on the faces of these kids, most of whom have never even been on an airplane, to see brothers in their pilots' uniforms. After all, only one percent of all pilots who fly commercial airplanes in the United States are African American.

"You need a camera to capture the thrilled reactions of these young people when we get to take them up in one of our 747's and fly to a place like Washington, D.C., or the Kennedy Space Center. Watching their joy is like seeing a whole new world being born."

You, as a mentor, have a unique opportunity not only to witness the birth of new worlds—or dreams—in your mentees but also to guide them toward reaching their dreams. And for young people that can make all the difference between idolizing heroes and becoming heroes in their own lives.

"I am small—five feet, eight inches, one hundred eighty-five pounds," says former New York Jets player Bruce Harper. "No one that small plays in the National Football League. On top of that, I came from a small college. But I had people who believed in me, who encouraged me all along the way.

"For athletes, coaches are very important people. Coaches ask you to stretch further than you think you can go. Your dad asks you to clean your room, walk the dog, and so on. But your coach challenges you to do the best and be better than you ever thought you could.

"I loved my coaches, both high school and college. My college coach, George Baldwin, was a legend. He went beyond the playing field. He cared about us, believed in us. And if he, whom we loved, believed in us, then we knew that we also had to believe in ourselves.

"His opinion of me mattered so much. I never wanted to let him down. His belief in me is what inspired me to get as far in my career as I did."

Mentors and role models play crucial parts in helping a young person reach their full potential. Oleta Adams, the international recording artist, who gave a concert at the 1999 national conference of the 100 Black Men of America in Detroit, put it this way: "The reason I am standing up here before you is because I had a mentor. Someone who was willing to give time—a lot of time, over a long period of time—to help me get to where I am. To teach me how to sing, how to make it in the business, how to hold myself—hold my head up, not just as a black woman but as a human being.

"That is how we are going to save all our children—black, brown, yellow, red, you name it—by being there for them. By serving as mentors and role models. God bless this endeavor and everyone who gives time to children."

Mentoring programs do not have to be highly structured to be successful. Our Long Island chapter achieves tremendous results through a program of informal exploration into the world of work. Every Saturday, one of the chapter's members takes a group of 15 to 20 young people to a local place of business for an in-depth, behind-the-scenes visit.

"Kids have the chance to see people who look like them and how they work," explains Lyndon L. Campbell, president and CEO of Lycam International, Inc., and vice president for programs of the 100 Black Men of Long Island. "We encourage them to choose as role models not just the celebrities they see on television but also to look to regular people they can identify with. We bring these young people in to talk to mechanics, magazine publishers, store owners, real estate agents, home builders, you name it.

"I like to quote to the kids what Dr. King said about work: 'If a man is called to be a street sweeper, he should sweep streets even as Michelangelo painted, or Beethoven composed music, or Shakespeare wrote poetry. He should sweep streets so well that all the hosts of heaven and earth will pause to say, here lived a great street sweeper who did his job well.' That is what we try to communicate to the kids. Find out what you want to do and learn to do it well.

"It is so easy for young people to get confused. They get to see so little of the real world and too much of the media. I recently took a group of mentees to a local car dealership for one of our Saturday expeditions. On the way over, I asked them all what they wanted to be, and this one kid said he was going to be either a bank manager or a rap star. Well, that is quite a range of ambitions.

"I said to him: 'Look, it's all right to dream big. But don't get yourself all confused. It is hard to work toward a concrete goal when you are all over the place.'

"It was a great excursion. The kids were all between eleven and fifteen, and their eyes just lit up when they saw all those shiny new cars. They spent a long time in the showroom, walking around, sitting in the cars, looking under the hoods. Then slowly, slowly, the kids started paying attention to the business of selling and maintaining cars. They listened to the managers and salespeople talk to customers, looked at the inventory of parts, and asked questions about how the ordering is done. They walked over to the used-car lot and talked to the manager about buying and selling cars. They went to the maintenance department, watched the mechanics work, and admired all the sophisticated tools and equipment. They looked at the computer system, the catalogs, the order forms, the contracts. The more they saw, the more interested they became in the details.

"It was amazing. Suddenly, what might seem like a ho-hum business to you and me was the coolest thing in the world to these kids. That, to me, is the real success of our mentoring program. Every week, we help our kids discover and explore something new. We encourage them to think about the choices they have in life, about the decisions they need to make to shape their futures. The payoff is in the process because *we* become the role models our children look up to instead of the inaccessible super-star athletes, rappers, and actors.

"The success of our program on Long Island was really driven home to me recently when I met a young man who was mentored by our chapter. He is twenty-four years old and is teaching in a local public school. When he told me about his career choice, I responded, 'Great. We need more African American men to make that kind of commitment.'

"He looked at me and said, 'I learned from my mentors at the 100 to choose a career that would allow me to do service for the community. I figure, you get, and you give back.' His answer pretty much sums up what mentoring is about and why it works."

Even Mentors Need Mentors

We have a saying in the 100 that success is not a destination, it is a journey. In other words, none of us is the person we are going to be for the rest of our lives. We are all works-in-progress. We are all always in the process of "becoming."

It is often hard for children to understand this. To them, the whole notion of growing up can look like moving from the constant change and uncertainty of childhood to the perceived stability and control of adulthood. It is as if you go from an incomplete person to a complete one, and that's that. You are done, and little changes after that.

As mentors, we have the important job of helping kids to understand and embrace the lifelong changes that are part of our development as human beings. The message we need to communicate to them is that they need to accept and take pride in themselves at every stage in their lives. Melba Patillo, who was one of the nine teenagers who integrated Little Rock's Central High School in 1957, tells her granddaughter India Annette Peyton, "God loves you, child. No matter what, he sees you as his precious idea."

Byron Hunt won his Super Bowl ring with the New York Giants in 1986. He says: "As an athlete, you never want to think about that last day. You've only lived one-third of your life when you finish your playing days, and there's a low that affects you and your family for quite a long time.

"Your life does not end with your athletic career, of course. It is really just beginning. But you've got to be prepared for that change.

"The sad thing is that about seventy percent of football

players do not have their college degrees. Unless you know the importance of education and the importance of it, you can't aspire to it. It's like if you only eat beans and rice all day. That's all you know, and you can't even wish for or desire a varied diet.

"The more you can imagine a positive, productive future for yourself after you stop playing, the better you feel about yourself. I am now trying to create a way for former athletes to get that positive feeling in their lives. We are bringing together ball players who have retired in a support and networking group. There are pro and college athletes. We go into the school systems and colleges and tell young people about our lives in and out of sports.

"When you are playing, you're always looking for something to inspire you. You get that same feeling from sharing your experience with young people. It takes the edge off that feeling that you can't still do what you had loved doing. It helps you see that there is a purpose and a place in the world for you. That's a real gift."

There are ups and downs in all our lives. The key to success is finding people at each turn of the road who believe that you are God's "precious idea" and who will stand by you and guide you on your journey. That is a lesson that we must impart to our mentees. Mentoring does not end when you graduate high school or college, or when you get your first job, or when you achieve the professional goal you set for yourself. Mentoring is a lifelong proposition, but it is up to *you* to seek out your mentors and ask for their guidance.

"I've had a mentor since I could walk!" laughs Jane E. Smith, Ed.D., president and CEO of the National Council of Negro Women, Inc. "Growing up in Atlanta, I would observe. And I would go up to women and ask them to be my mentors.

"I remember in second grade, I had a teacher that I really looked up to. She was so dignified and prepared. She made us want to learn, because she cared about us. I wanted so much to be like her. So I approached her and asked, 'Why are you so wonderful? How did you get to be this way?' In my way, I was asking her to mentor me.

"I also looked up to my grandmother as a mentor. She was the first African American to have an office in City Hall in Atlanta. An educator, she had focus, discipline, truth, honesty, and a strong work ethic. I learned so much from her.

"My grandmother and my school principal. I knew I wanted to be like them. In high school, I went to the principal and asked her if I could accompany her on trips to learn how the education system worked.

"And it was like that all along the road for me. I went on to Spelman College, where I was a Whitney Young and Woodrow Wilson Fellow and served as assistant to the president. I earned my Master's in Sociology from Emory University and a Doctorate in Education and Social Policy Analysis from Harvard. I could not have done these things if I had not had caring, dedicated people who were willing to help me along the way.

"And in my professional life, I have continued to find mentors and to draw inspiration from those who have come before me, in order to serve my community to my full potential. After finishing my doctorate degree, I was named the first managing director of the Atlanta and Detroit affiliates of INROADS, a career development organization for minority students. In 1991, I became director of development for the New Direction Team of the Martin Luther King, Jr., Center for Nonviolent Social Change, and then served as director of the Carter Center's Atlanta Project, working to improve the quality of life on the neighborhood level.

"In 1998, I became president and CEO of the National Council of Negro Women. The organization was founded in 1935, and now has two-hundred-and-fifty community-based sections and eighty thousand members. We reach out to four million women throughout the nation and in Africa. And have mentoring programs for both girls and boys.

"I am following in the tradition of past presidents, Dr. Dorothy Height and Mary McLeod Bethune. These were women of substance and presence. They had character. They and their legacy mentor me.

"Mentoring is important in the tradition of our community. But whereas I could always reach out and ask to be mentored, a lot of people—and children especially—cannot ask for the help they need. They are too shy or do not have the necessary language. That is why it is so important that we reach out to young people first, whether through formal mentoring programs or individually. Once we reach these kids, we can show them how to continue to reach out for mentors throughout their lives and how to mentor others."

The best way to show your mentees the continuum of mentoring is to share with them your own experiences of being mentored. You can start by talking about the people who were important in guiding your development as a child. Maybe you have a barber shop story or a memory of a favorite aunt or teacher or coach. Maybe you were in Big Brothers/Big Sisters or the Boys Club or Girls Club. Talk about the different stages you went through in your life and the people who have been there for you during those times. If you feel comfortable, introduce your mentees to someone who is a mentor to you now. The idea that the adult whom they look up to and turn to for help also needs guidance and support will help kids feel empowered and will strengthen the bond between you.

There is a Yoruba proverb that says, "It is the needle that pulls the thread." We are all threads in the fabric of our community, and our collective future is the needle that pulls us toward ever greater achievements.

The "Movement of Youth" mentoring program of the 100 Black Men of Greater Charlotte chapter is a structured mentoring program for 70 at-risk middle and high school students between the ages of 11 and 15. Most of the young people are from households headed by single females and are marginal to above average academic performers.

This comprehensive program includes:

- One-on-one individual mentoring.
- *Saturday Academy:* For six hours every month, the young people are exposed to workshops taught by experts on such subjects as communication skills, drug abuse awareness, academic and cultural issues, computer training, male/female relationships, chess, scuba diving, rock climbing, and so on.
- *Tutorial program:* Six hours of educational tutorial services are held each week. The classes are conducted by certified teachers who are trained to help young people having difficulty with their schoolwork or who want to improve their classroom performance.

- *Tracking and monitoring:* Students in grades nine through twelve are systematically tracked and monitored by the program for academic, social, and cultural progress. They are also evaluated by adult monitors in each school who complete profiles and progress reports on each student.

- *Charlotte Youth Connection:* Young people participate in this service learning program that unites youths from the city's different socioeconomic and ethnic backgrounds. The program is designed for teenage boys and girls to gain volunteer experience at area agencies, and they are encouraged to develop volunteer projects to benefit their own community.

- *Scholarships:* Students in the mentoring program who graduate with a 3.0 grade point average or higher are awarded a $10,000 scholarship; those with a grade point average between 2.0 and 2.9 receive $3,000. The current scholarship commitment is $84,000; by the year 2000, it is projected to be $203,000.

According to chapter president Kevin Patterson, the importance of a community-based mentoring program such as "Movement of Youth" is that it provides a vital link between positive adult African American males and young people.

"Our adult role models are constructive influences for inspiring and redirecting African American males who are at risk of becoming dropouts, being impoverished, or being incarcerated as adults," he says. "We don't want them to leave school before receiving a degree. Our commitment is to help these young men develop a sense of self-worth and pride that is critical for overcoming the many societal barriers that will challenge them along the way."

With such vision and commitment, it is not surprising that the accomplishments of the program for 1998–99 were so remarkable:

- Eleven of 12 graduating seniors entered college in the fall of 1999.
- The grade point average for seniors was up 20 percent.
- The school days missed were down 46 percent.
- The chess team from the program finished second in the North Carolina Scholastic Chess Tournament. The same team finished 33 out of 66 teams at the National Finals held in Arizona in 1998.
- In 1999, 20 students who had been mentored in the program were enrolled in colleges across the southeast.

Building Character

"One of the most powerful experiences I've had around mentoring was my first meeting with my current mentee," recounts Randy Walker from the Detroit 100. "On his application, he wrote that he wanted to be mentored by a white man. When I sat down with him and the counselor from Big Brothers/Big Sisters, our mentoring partner here in Detroit, we asked him why he wanted to be matched up with a white man. You know what he said? 'They are honest, and they have good jobs.'

"Just like that. And mind you, this is an eight-year-old kid. It nearly knocked the wind out of me. If that's what he thinks about black men, then what does he think about himself? What kind of future does he imagine for himself?

"I was really shaken. But I was also determined to help this young African American boy see that black men had integrity, brains, good jobs. That it wasn't color that determined your character.

"It was that experience that really drove home for me the real purpose of mentoring: to build character in our young people. And the only way to do that is to model what it means to have character."

That means that what you do—the way you conduct yourself, the language you use, the choices you make—assumes a special importance. It is not enough to tell a young boy or girl that being on time is a sign of responsibility and respect; for instance, you must reinforce the notion by being punctual yourself.

Use your behavior to promote learning and positive development in your mentees. If you want to encourage them to read, read with them at every opportunity. If you want to teach them that it is important to take care of one's well-being, set an example by walking up a couple of flights of stairs instead of taking an elevator. And always discuss with your mentees why you make your choices.

If you are going somewhere together, take public transportation, so your mentee will be able to get there on his or her own in the future. Take some extra time beforehand to research the transportation alternatives together by calling your local public transportation authority. In this way, you will teach life skills and start to build your mentee's sense of self-reliance.

"I had a college English teacher, Dr. Maggie Brown

Daniels," says Dwayne Ashley, now the executive director of the Thurgood Marshall Scholarship Fund. "She was in her eighties when I got to school, and she would always say, 'Writing well is the most important skill you can have.'

"And she meant it. She made me conjugate every verb over and over until I got them right and helped me learn proper grammar so that I could become a good writer.

"When I graduated, Dr. Daniels gave me a card that said: 'I wish you well in all your undertakings.' I was so awed by that word, *undertakings.* It made an enormous impression on me that she considered my future of such importance. And I had so much respect for her and the way she used words that I could not help but give more weight to where I was headed.

"I still keep that card in my office as a reminder that my life is an undertaking. I always feel this funny mixture of pride and responsibility when I look at it. And I try to pass its message on to the young people I mentor now."

The power of a mentor to build character is far-reaching. By finding creative solutions to challenges your mentees face, you can teach resourcefulness—the skills of finding and weighing alternatives. By engaging kids in discussions of the choices you make, you can teach critical thinking skills. The opportunities for modeling and teaching are boundless, but you have to be committed to remaining conscious and purposeful in your relationships with your mentees.

"I'm the product of a single-mother household," says Tupac Hunter of the Detroit chapter of the 100. "And I'm a living example of the importance of a strong, positive male role model.

"My father wasn't around, but my mother had a friend who was an executive at Ford. Whenever he came to my house, he took special care to talk to me, tell me about his job, ask me about school and my hobbies. There was this way about him, like he was really in charge.

"I loved that about him. I liked how he held himself, what he wore, how he spoke. I mentor because I realize the impact this man had on my life. And I try to mentor in that self-possessed, positive way that he went about being a role model for me."

Ultimately, we all want to pass down a certain part of ourselves to future generations, through our own children, through the children we mentor. The important thing is to be clear with yourself about what it is that you value enough in your own character that you want to encourage in the characters of young people. There are lots of ways of doing that. You can look in the mirror and ask yourself what of your reflection you would want to see in your mentee. You can sit down with a piece of paper and write down the five traits that you consider your best. You can ask several people whose opinion you care about to talk with you about what part they value in you.

"My main purpose is to lead a life that leaves behind something with others," explains Dr. Jane Smith. "I want to impress on young people how important it is to have high standards in their lives and to have faith in their talents and gifts."

Each of us owes it to the young people we will be working with—and to ourselves—to be purposeful in what we choose to model for them. For, as a Kenyan proverb says, "The world was not given to us by our parents, it was lent to us by our children."

What You Can Do:

1. Recall the important role models in your life.
2. Determine what values you would like to communicate to a young person.
3. Consult with your own mentors about becoming an effective role model.

CHAPTER FIVE

Balancing Heart and Mind: The Five Stages of the Mentoring Relationship

Being a friend means mastering the art of timing. There is a time for silence. And a time to let go and allow people to hurl themselves into their own history. And a time to pick up the pieces when it's all over.

—GLORIA NAYLOR

All too often in the beginning of a mentoring relationship, the heart tells you that you will completely change a young person's life. You project your own expectations and hopes onto your mentee—hopes and expectations that may not be realistic in the context of the child's life. This is where the mind needs to balance out the heart. You need to combine reality and expectations into a well-defined plan. Remember, a mentor is not a savior but a trusted friend. Let reality be your guide. The probability of success is always enhanced when heart and mind are balanced.

Mentoring is an undertaking, a journey. You begin with a desire to give back, to get involved, to make a difference in the lives of young people. Then, you become a mentor to a child—a boy or a girl with a history that is unique, who has expectations, talents, fears—and suddenly you realize you really care about this particular child. A relationship is in the making, and you have set off on a journey.

At first, there are the tentative steps of getting to know each other. Then come the tests of establishing ground rules for the relationship and building trust. As the bond between you and your mentee grows stronger, you begin to explore the world together and learn from each other. As you do so, deep regard and affection develops between you. In time, this engenders true understanding and lifelong trust.

There are, of course, as in any relationship, places where things can go wrong between you and your mentee. However, if you understand the dynamics of the mentoring relationship and the various stages of its development, you will be well prepared to face the challenges you might encounter. That is what we mean by balancing heart and mind. Caring and empathy are essential to succeeding as a mentor, but so is being informed, aware, and thoughtful.

One of the most important findings that came out of the research study that the Gallup Organization conducted on the mentoring programs of the 100 Black Men of America was a clear picture of the evolution of a mentoring relationship and the skills a mentor must exercise to make each successful. The study showed that a mentoring relationship grows through the following five stages:

ONE: Helping the mentee grow

TWO: Expanding opportunities for the mentee

THREE: Learning together

FOUR: Investing in the future of the mentee

FIVE: Trusting each other

These stages are a continuum—each building on the previous one to deepen the bond between you and your mentee. It is especially important that you understand this aspect of the mentoring relationship. Rushing through one stage to get to another or trying to leapfrog over any of them will only get you frustrated and may undermine your connection with your mentee. Growth takes time, and you will need to be patient.

In the pages that follow, we will look at each of the stages of the mentoring relationship. This is intended as a framework that will help you think about and structure your own mentoring experience. Each relationship is unique, and you need to listen carefully for the rhythm you and your mentee share. That, more than anything else, will guide you through the exciting and deeply satisfying process of building your relationship.

Stage One: Helping the Mentee Grow

"We didn't call it mentoring back when I was growing up in Johnstown, South Carolina," recalls Lenny Springs, founding president of the 100 Black Men of Charlotte. "It was the family, community, neighbors, church. Everybody had their eyes on you and their arms around you.

"It was my grandmother who encouraged me to get off the farm and get an education. When I was away at college, she used to send me these letters; there was always a dollar and words of encouragement. I loved those letters. They made me feel like I could do anything.

"That's the thing with young people. You've got to let them know that you are there to support them, to help them feel safe enough and confident enough to find out what's outside of their own little environment and community. It's all about caring and exposure."

The first stage of the mentoring relationship can be very fragile. You and the young person you are working with do not know each other. Meetings and conversations can seem strained, with you doing most of the talking. This is the time when you must show genuine interest in your mentee. Find out about the young person's interests and dreams. Talk about setting goals. Most important, express your satisfaction with seeing your mentee grow and develop, no matter how small the changes. That is the best way to demonstrate that you care.

"I've had a mentor through the 100 since I was thirteen," says fifteen-year-old Donnell Goode, a mentee of the 100's Cleveland, Tennessee, chapter. Donnell, who was selected as the chapter's 1999 Mentee of the Year, says: "I live with my mother and sister, and it was my mom who suggested that I join the mentoring program. I had no idea what a mentor was, so I didn't know what to expect.

"We started having meetings at Cleveland State University. I was not good at reading. My mentor, who is a lawyer, figured that out right away, and he began reading with me, helping me to read better. He just kept saying, 'You can do it, Donnell. Go slow, and you'll get it.' Well, I still would rather be out playing ball, but I'm a pretty good reader.

"Once the reading was going well, my mentor asked me if I wanted to learn how to work a computer. I was nervous, you know, but he just said, 'Come on, it's like playing a game.' And he showed me all the different programs, how to write on it, how to draw. It was fun, and now I can use it for school.

"I've changed a lot since I met my mentor. I've met a lot of different people and have been to all kinds of events. I even went to the national convention of the 100 in Detroit. That was really cool to see so many really successful black men who care about kids like me and to get to spend time with other young people from all over.

"My mentor is always there for me, and I try to live up to my side of the deal. I show up for our meetings on time. I try to do what he asks me to do. I am studying more. And I definitely think more about my education and my future.

"It's a good feeling to know that my mentor cares enough to want to help me. I am going to do the same one day, help kids the way he helps me."

Nurturing is the foundation of successful mentoring, and the first stage of the relationship has to set the tone between you and the young person you are mentoring. This is the time when you should begin to establish yourself as a role model for your mentee. Talk about your values and back them up with consistent actions. Help your mentee think about what is right and what is wrong. If the young person acts in a way you do not approve of, discuss it and point out more appropriate behavior. Listen to your mentee, encourage him or her to think about the future, and help to set realistic and attainable goals. The objective at this stage is for you and your mentee to make a strong commitment to the future.

"I have this friend," says Casarae Lattimore, another mentee from the Cleveland, Tennessee, chapter of the 100. "I've known him for quite a long time. His name is Andrew Johnson, and he is my mentor.

"I started hanging out with him when I was about twelve. He took me to major league baseball games and college football games. He was also the one who took me on my first plane ride. That was the most terrible experience in my whole life.

"Nobody told me how the ride would be in a six-passenger Cessna airplane. I just got a call from Andrew one morning at eight asking me if I wanted to go down to the Chattanooga Metro Airport for a plane ride with a group of kids. As soon as I got off the phone, I started to regret saying 'yes.' I was scared in the car all the way down to Chattanooga, and things didn't get any better when we got down there.

"We sat in a small lobby, waiting for the airplane to return from its test flight. It had been having problems that morning. I was so nervous just sitting there, I ate four doughnuts and drank three cups of juice. So I was feeling sick even before we got on the plane.

"When the plane was ready, we climbed in, buckled up our safety belts, and got ready to fly. The pilot cranked up the engine, and it sounded just like a giant lawn mower. I wanted to jump out right then and there, but it was too late. We were already heading for the runway.

"Once in the air, the plane got even louder. I was so scared, my head hurt and my stomach kept flipping over. I held the air sickness bag in my lap the whole ride, and every time we hit an air pocket—and let me tell you, there were lots of them—I grabbed on to the seat in front of me for dear life.

"When it was finally over, I promised myself that I would never do that again. On the way home, Andrew and I talked about being scared and how there are lots of things you've got to face in life that are frightening. But you can also pick and choose what makes you comfortable and you shouldn't be ashamed of your fears.

"Andrew helps me a lot. He has a way of looking at things that makes me learn something. When I was younger and had problems at school, he helped me through them. He still gives me a hand with my schoolwork. And if he can't be there for me, he makes sure to find someone who can. He has been a great influence on my life."

Helping the mentee grow is an essential first step in the mentoring relationship. To be successful during this stage, you must derive genuine satisfaction from watching your mentee experiment, change, and develop. If you do not, you may enjoy spending time with the young person, but you will not be effective at encouraging growth. And the young person you are mentoring will most likely feel that you do not really care about him or her. Therefore, listen to your heart carefully as you undergo this delicate stage of mentoring.

Stage Two: Expanding Opportunities for the Mentee

"I have a dream for myself," says Jannelle, a Philadelphia native, who is now a sophomore at the University of Pennsylvania. "I want to be a Supreme Court Justice someday. My role model is Thurgood Marshall and I decided in junior high school that I wanted to be like him so I could also help others.

"I will never forget the expression on my mother's face when I told her about my plans for going to law school. 'Child,' she said, 'how are you going to do that? We'll be lucky if we can afford to send you to college.' It's not that she was trying to be discouraging, either. She really couldn't see how I could possibly ever get there.

"And other people just plain laughed at me: 'Oh, yeah, they're just going to roll out the red carpet for you.' Frankly, I did not see what was so funny. I just got angry and frustrated. I knew what I wanted, but I didn't have the faintest idea of what to do to get a shot at realizing my dream. And nobody seemed to want to help me figure it out.

"Mrs. Peters, my social studies teacher, saved the day. She suggested that I enroll in the new mentoring program that had been set up at the school by a group of local companies at the beginning of that year. I figured it was worth a shot and filled out an application. In the place where they asked what I was looking for in a mentor, I wrote that I wanted someone sensitive.

"A couple of weeks later, I met with the coordinator of the program and with Jim, a warehouse manager at a small manufacturing firm who had been assigned as my mentor. I was kind of put off at first. How was this guy going to help me? But he had this really nice way of listening, with his head tilted to the side, that made me feel comfortable. We agreed to give it a try.

"The first time we met for real, Jim asked me all kinds of questions, told me about himself, basically just chitchatted. Then, he got kind of quiet, squinted at me, and said, 'On your application, you wrote that you wanted to have a mentor who is sensitive. What does that mean to you?' 'Somebody who listens,' I answered. 'Oh, I see,' he said. And we left it at that.

"Just as he was about to drop me off at home, Jim asked me if I had any plans about what I wanted to do in life. I told him about Thurgood Marshall and how I also wanted to be on the Supreme Court. He looked at me very seriously and said that he thought it was a great idea. I thought he might be putting me on, but the next time we met, he suggested we go to the library and look up some books about the Court. We spent the next three hours reading about its history, the people who had served on it, its customs and procedures. It was great to learn so much. And it was especially great to be taken seriously.

"Over the next months, Jim did everything he could to encourage and help me. He came by school and talked to my teachers and guidance counselors. He visited my house and spoke with my mom. He helped me research colleges and scholarships. He introduced me to the lawyer his company used, who put me in touch with people she had gone to law school with. Through one of the contacts, I got a summer internship at a law firm downtown. Suddenly, I did not just have a dream, I had the beginnings of a plan of how to make it happen.

"The best part, though, was the visit to the Supreme

Court. Jim talked with the mentoring program coordinator, and somehow they figured out a way to get a few of the mentors and us kids to be able to get into the visitors' gallery during one of the sessions. That was simply awesome, actually to be there in person and to picture myself on that bench.

"It's an amazing feeling to have someone believe in you and help pave the way. It makes everything seem possible. And I am so proud now when I speak to Jim on the phone and tell him about the classes I am taking and everything else I am doing. I feel like it's an opportunity to let him know that his trust and support are paying off. It is really important to me to have him be proud of who I am becoming."

The second stage of the mentoring relationship builds on the nurturing bond established in the first stage by expanding the mentee's opportunities for success. During this time, you need to show the young person that you are committed to helping him or her accomplish long-term goals. The point is not to "do" for the youth, but to open doors in order to facilitate further learning and growth.

This is the time when you need to learn as much as possible about the young person's environment. Talk regularly with your mentee's parents and enlist their support for the mentoring process. Visit teachers, counselors, community, and religious leaders—anyone who plays a significant part in your mentee's life. The message is: This kid's future is all of our responsibility, and it depends on us pulling together and creating a safety net, a community. And into this community, bring new people by introducing the young person to your friends, business associates, people who do the kind of work the kid is interested in. The goal is to create a miniature "village" around your mentee, one that will support his or her growth, development, and dreams.

If you believe that young people should learn by solving their own problems or taking their "lumps," you might find it difficult to become really involved in your mentee's life. In that case, chances are that your relationship will remain superficial and will begin to feel unproductive. Should that happen, it might be time to reexamine your reasons for wanting to mentor.

Stage Three: Learning Together

It's important to remember that you have to be confident you have something valuable to offer to a young person in order to make a commitment to being involved in your mentee's life. As your relationship moves through the second stage of development, that confidence is likely to grow as you see firsthand how much of a difference you are making. What is also likely to happen is that you will begin to realize that your mentee is not the only one who is changing—that the relationship is giving you a new perspective on things, that you, too, are learning. At the point you begin to see yourself and your mentee as learning partners, you'll know that you've entered the third stage of the mentoring relationship.

"When Willie and I were first matched up through the program, I was worried about our compatibility," recalls Daniel, a New York advertising executive who mentors through a community center in Brooklyn. "We had such different interests. He lives and breathes music. Me, I don't know the first thing about it. I expressed my concern to the people at the center, but they encouraged me to give it a try. I can't tell you how happy I am that I did.

"The first few months we spent just getting to know each other. We would go for walks in the park, see movies, talk. I asked Willie about the music he liked, and he introduced me to the blues. That's his thing. He wants to be a blues guitarist. 'Like Muddy Waters,' he says. And when he played for me, I was truly impressed.

"We also worked on his studies. He spent so much time practicing, sometimes his homework went undone. And the grades reflected that. I pressed him to find a balance, to make sure that his academics were good enough to get him into a music school. That was tough, because he had this romantic vision of simply breaking through, the way his heroes had done.

"I found some contacts at a music company through my agency and introduced Willie to people who were actually making records. We went to a couple of studios, talked to session musicians and to engineers. What turned it around for Willie was a conversation with a keyboard player. 'Hey,' he said, 'you might not learn to play any better at a school, but you'll make contacts for a lifetime.' That really sank in, and our future conversations about school turned to questions about different programs and scholarships.

"But the critical point for me came when I got tickets for the two of us to go see *It Ain't Nothing but the Blues*, a musical history of blues in America. That really captured my imagination and helped me understand Willie's fascination with the genre. The play was filled with overwhelming emotion, humor, and poignancy. And I wanted to know more.

"Willie became my guide. He knew so much of the

music, and we explored its origins together. We read liner notes, books, magazines. And the more we read, the broader we went—into gospel, jazz, rock. Through the music, we were both learning about a part of history that our textbooks had not taught us. That became a real bond, this mutual discovery."

The point is to remain open to satisfaction beyond that of doing good. In spending time with a young person, you will most likely find new ways of looking at things, new ideas, new interests. If you have the confidence to learn from the young person or people in your life, you will be enriched by the relationship. And in learning from and with your mentee, you will reinforce his or her strengths and talents.

If, on the other hand, you have a fairly rigid idea of how the relationship is supposed to work—that you are there to help the mentee grow and not the other way around—you might cut off opportunities for growth and limit your own effectiveness. In case you find yourself in such a position, it might be worthwhile to ask for some support and guidance from the program through which you are mentoring or from your own mentor.

Being a mentor is an ongoing learning process. Formal mentoring is evolving, and new strategies and techniques are being continuously developed. Stay connected, keep current, hone your skills. What works today may not be so effective tomorrow.

Stage Four: Investing in the Future of the Mentee

Mentoring, as we have seen in talking about the first three stages of this special relationship, is the process of investing more and more of yourself into assuring a young person's future. That investment can take many forms—everything from sharing your knowledge and values to helping create opportunities for learning and success.

There does come a point, however, when the investment takes on a different tone. It goes beyond caring and spending long periods of time with your mentee. Usually, this deeper level of investment takes the shape of the mentor's bringing the mentee into his or her own family or becoming a part of the mentee's family. Of course, this does not mean that you adopt each other. You simply acknowledge that you have become integral parts of one another's lives.

"I have two boys of my own," says Randy Walker of the Detroit 100. "I thought it would be a good idea to have a mentee who is the same age as my older son, you know, to have a strong family connection. We started doing things together every Saturday, the three boys and I. Movies. Short trips. Games.

"At first, things seemed to go pretty well. But then I began to notice that there was more and more friction between the two older kids. My son would often get impatient and angry, and my mentee would get sullen and withdrawn. Fights would erupt about what movie to go to or where they wanted to eat. It was turning into a real power struggle.

"What started out as my attempt to expand our family was quickly turning into a disruptive problem. Even my wife began to complain about the negative effect all of this was having on our lives.

"Finally, I knew that we needed to get some help to sort things out. We all sat down with a social worker and talked. With help from the counselor, each of the boys articulated what was going on. My son complained that my mentee did not share his interest in sports and that the time we all spent together ate into our private time. My mentee said that he wanted more of my time; he wanted me to pay more attention to him.

"It made sense. I had brought my mentee into the family without first establishing a real relationship with him, so there was confusion and competition from the start. Clearly, I needed to make some changes. I just hoped that things hadn't gotten to the point where I couldn't turn them around.

"I talked to each of the boys individually and explained that it was still important to me to have all of us do things together, but that I understood their feelings and would like to try a different way of structuring our time together. I began to see my mentee every other Saturday, and on those days would pick him up by myself. We would talk about his schoolwork, his interests—whatever he wanted to talk about. And then we would go and pick up my sons and go do some sort of activity together.

"It's been two years now, and my relationship with my mentee is really strong. The time that we spend alone together is very important to both of us. It has allowed us to establish a solid bond. I enjoy seeing him grow, and he, for his part, appreciates my commitment to the relationship. And he is becoming part of my family. The boys still squabble occasionally, like ten-year-olds will, but there isn't all that friction.

"I tell you, I think we all learned so much from this whole experience. With kids, you have to be so mindful, whether you are raising them, mentoring them, caring for them, or teaching them. You've got to check that ego at the door and listen, listen really carefully."

The mentoring relationship is a delicate one. You must constantly remain focused on maintaining the balance between your feelings for the youth you are working with and the boundaries necessary to make the relationship successful. This is especially important when you begin to involve your family and that of your mentee. You need to be conscious of the fact that your relationship with your mentee can be equally threatening, although for different reasons, to members of both your families. Therefore, as you move into the investing stage, be sure to carefully monitor all the dynamics and, most important, do not rush things.

"My father has always been a role model for me," says Lee Bush, who was mentored by the 100's Jackson, Mississippi, chapter, and who is now attending Morehouse College and plans to go into investment banking. "But I have to admit, I was a little jealous when he started mentoring Robert. 'Why is he spending so much time with him?' I kept thinking.

"The thing that helped me was that I was in the mentoring program, too. I knew what it was all about. And I saw my dad interacting with Robert, saw how special that relationship was. I also saw how important it was for Robert, what it meant to him.

"By the time we were juniors in high school, we were best friends, like brothers. We still are. We are here at Morehouse together. And now we mentor each other in our own particular way: He does a lot of public speaking to young people, and I work with elementary school kids. It's great to be able to give back, to feel a part of something so powerful."

There are unique challenges in the investing stage of the mentoring relationship, just as there are all along the way. The rewards, however, are well worth it. The relationship grows, expands, the caring bond between you and your mentee extends to other important people in your lives.

"My son Casarae started being mentored three years ago," says Patricia Lattimore, whose son is a mentee at the 100 Black Men of Cleveland, Tennessee. "I wanted him to have a father figure in his life. I can talk to him about a lot of things, but he needs to talk to a man. And he's loved being around an older man, learning from him.

"So I don't have any jealousy. Just the opposite, all I feel is gratitude. On Father's Day, I gave Andrew—Casarae's mentor—a card, saying, 'You may not be my son's father, but you are like one to him. Thank you.' I also tell Andrew's wife how much I appreciate what she does for Casarae, how they've welcomed him into their home.

"As a parent, you can't be greedy about the love of your child. You've got to share it."

Stage Five: Trusting Each Other

"When I told my academic advisor at Amherst that I was apprehensive about going to Cambridge University to do graduate work," says Melvin Rogers, who was mentored by the New York chapter, "he told me: 'You become great by stepping out into nothingness.'

"That really stuck with me. I kept thinking about all the times I had been afraid, of all the things I had done to get to where I was. I am a kid from the Bronx, right, who had attended Grace Dodge Public High School, and here I was graduating from Amherst with a Phi Beta Kappa and on my way to England to study at Cambridge. So the feeling of stepping out into nothingness was not new to me. What I had to remember was what had helped me take those steps. And that was knowing that I had the confidence of my mentor and the whole of the One Hundred behind me.

"That's what I get out of being mentored, I never feel alone. I know that there are people who will back me up, who will be there when I need advice or help, who will help me confront fears and obstacles. Knowing that, there isn't anything I cannot do."

Mutual trust is a critical ingredient of a successful mentoring relationship. All along the way, you and your mentee will negotiate and renegotiate agreements, ground rules, boundaries. You will test each other and the strength of your connection. Through this process, you will build an understanding and respect that will affect both of your lives.

Many mentors describe this stage of the mentoring relationship as the point at which they begin to feel that they and the young people they mentor will be friends forever. The unconditional acceptance and support of such a friendship will become a resource your mentee can call upon long after the formal relationship is over. You and the young person will have been transformed, and you will carry one another in your hearts for the rest of your lives.

"I knew it was time to go," says Althea, a senior at a New York City community college, who had been mentored through a program in her high school. "The four years I had Lydia as my mentor were such a special time. I had learned so much, seen so much. She'd become like an older sister to me. But I was out of high school, and I needed to go off on my own.

"As hard as it was not to have her be part of my life, it was a really important step. I had to prove that I could make it on my own. And I did, but with Lydia as my secret weapon. Whenever I came up against a difficult situation, I'd hear her voice. It was like I had taken a part of her with me. That's how I think about it—everything she gave me is inside me. I feel so blessed by that.

"I know that someday, when the time is right, I will see her again. I will pick up the phone, call her, and ask her to dinner. I'll tell her about everything I've done. And I have no doubt that she will be as accepting of me as she has always been, that she will be proud of me. That makes me proud of myself, because I feel that I am living the life Lydia helped me imagine and strive for."

Mentoring is a journey, a road you and your mentee travel together to prepare the young person for the journeys that lie ahead. And when the time comes for your paths to diverge, you will carry with you the profound satisfaction of knowing you have truly earned a young person's unconditional regard.

What You Can Do:

1. Make sure the mutual expectations between you and your mentor are clearly defined.
2. Be patient in building a mentoring relationship.
3. Be flexible and accept the young person's unique personality.

CHAPTER SIX

Completing the Circle: The Continuum of Mentoring

I am we.

—AFRICAN AXIOM

Mentoring is a work of the heart. It is a desire to build community, to inspire hope, to share success, to enrich life. It is a special way to look at people and yourself, responsibility and accomplishment: It is an infectious passion that is passed on with each encouraging word, supportive pat on the back, and proud smile. Mentoring is a life-affirming circle that has the power to heal the wounds and divisions of our society and that expands every time two people touch each other's lives as mentor and mentee.

"We are all still being mentored," says Lenny Springs, founding president of the 100 Black Men of Charlotte. "If you look at each of us in the 100, someone in our lives recognized us, told us that we could achieve and be somebody. Success doesn't just happen. It's not the luck of the draw. We are all standing on other people's shoulders. And I can't forget that. I won't forget it. That's why I give back, because someone paved the way for me."

It is important that as a mentor you recognize that you and your mentee are part of a wider circle of support. Every one of us needs mentors throughout our lives—guides to help us deal with the changes, challenges, and uncertainties that come at every stage of the journey. Often, it takes a great deal of courage to ask for help. Knowing how to seek out mentors requires determination and skill.

As a mentor, you are a meaningful role model, with a profound effect on a young person's life. Your mentee will look to you to learn not only how to mentor others but also how to find mentors for him- or herself at various stages throughout life. Initiating young people into the circle of mentoring is as important as participating in it, and you need to give special attention to the attitudes and behaviors you pass on to them.

In this chapter we will take a look at how you can bring your own mentors into the lives of your mentees; how you can involve young people in mentoring others; and how you can help your mentees learn to find mentors throughout their lifetimes.

My Mentor's Mentor

"The man who taught me about mentoring was Dr. Thomas E. Poag," says Robert L. Stevenson, Ph.D., president of the 100 Black Men of Savannah, Georgia. "He was the first person to establish a full-fledged speech and drama department at a historically black college. That is where I met him, at Tennessee State College in Nashville.

"He had such a sense of commitment; he gave so much to his students. Dr. Poag did not just teach us, he took an active part in our lives. For me, he became not only an inspiration but also the bridge to success. I ran out of money in college and had to drop out. Dr. Poag made it possible for me to return by getting me an acting scholarship. When I wanted to enroll in the Master's program at Tennessee State, he guaranteed my loans out of his salary.

"I have patterned my career on his. When I became the first African American to get a Ph.D. in speech and drama from Cornell University, I felt like I was making good on all of Dr. Poag's trust and belief in me. It was one of the greatest days of my life. And as an educator, I have followed in his footsteps. I have been teaching English, speech, and theater at Savannah State University since 1965. In these thirty-five years, I have tried to pass on to all of my students my mentor's legacy.

"Dr. Poag taught me that you can never lose by doing the right thing. That is the precept I live by, and that is what I impress on my students. Good begets good, and it is our duty to share our good with our brothers and sisters. I see the effect this has on the young people I teach—I see them taking it in—and it does my heart proud to know that I am keeping Dr. Poag's spirit alive through my work."

In the African American community, there is a long tradition of passing on our successes, our beliefs, and our values from one generation to the next. It is a tradition of "lifting as we climb," in the words of the motto of the National Council of Negro Women.

"I believe that upward mobility is not just the result of your ability but of people pulling you up and helping you out," says Harry L. Coaxum, assistant vice president of franchising for the McDonald's Corporation and chairman of the board of directors of the 100 Black Men of Chicago.

"There have always been people who have been there for me and with me. A shoulder to lean on or an attentive ear—someone to provide advice and counsel. These individuals challenge your thinking, make you slow down and think about your situation. They do it because they know you can't get through life by yourself, that you need a support system.

"I joined McDonald's right after college. Clint Gulley was the supervisor on my first job with the company in Miami. He took a liking to me and came by the restaurant to talk, to help me out. When I got frustrated, he coached me through the process of navigating in the corporate culture and showed me that there would be bumps in the road. He gave me perspective.

"It was so important to me to have another African American man to talk to. It helped me deal with the loneliness and the alienation that I felt entering corporate America. To this day, Clint remains a really central role model for me.

"I mentor because people like Clint gave me their time and their caring. In my days, there was a lot more 'we';

now there is more 'I.' The pace is faster. There is less time to reach out and help the kid next door. Today, formal mentoring needs to take the place of the informal support that we had growing up."

A good way to share the importance of mentoring with your mentees is simply to talk about them. Tell the young people what it felt like to have a caring older person take you under his or her wing as you were starting out your career or how it was to become a parent or deal with the loss of your own parents. Tell them the stories your mentors told you; quote their favorite sayings; recollect special memories; recall important occasions. The idea is to make your mentors real for your mentees, to bring them into your relationship with the young people.

I always tell my mentees the story of Billy Latin, the handyman who prompted me to get my driver's license instead of settling for a learner's permit when I was sixteen. I also describe the barber shop in Toccoa. I want these young people to get the flavor of what it was like being a kid in my days, to be connected to the past.

"I grew up in New York City," says Dr. Thomas Minter, former Dean of Education at Lehman College of the City University of New York and the original founder of the mentoring program of the One Hundred Black Men, Inc., in New York City. "My family has been in education for many generations. I have many relatives in North Carolina who were school teachers. I remember how they mentored their students even into adulthood, how they didn't lose contact with them after graduation.

"This idea that you are mentored—and mentor—your whole life is very important and has helped me immensely. I have had mentors every step of the way. I was in the Boy

Scouts, went to different camps, belonged to church. I had people who told me when I was doing well and when I was not. It is necessary to have people show you the path, to give you a hand to walk the path, and then to help you maintain your way.

"When you remember those who have mentored you, you want to pass it on. In 1985—I was chair of the Education Committee of the One Hundred Black Men, Inc., at the time—I saw the need for a mentoring program. The purpose was to assist black junior and senior high school students by providing career orientation and motivation.

"As an educator, I know that young people model themselves after their parents, teachers, and elders. Mentoring was an idea whose time had come. Our group had a number of accomplished men who could expose young people to a variety of educational opportunities and career paths, to help them see what was open to them.

"Young people need someone just to sit down with them and point out the options and opportunities. They have to learn to be flexible and open to change and to be prepared. A mentor helps you to find and define your center, to set goals, and to articulate what you want to be in life.

"I like to tell young people the story of an incident that had a profound effect on my life. When I was a boy, I loved electric trains and was always playing with my train set. One day, a workman came to the house to repair something. He walked past my room and stopped to look at the trains. 'What do you want to be when you grow up?' he asked me. I said, 'A train man.' He got very excited at my response. 'I am so delighted that you want to be a trained man,' he beamed. I have never forgotten the pride and conviction with which he said that. To this day, I continue to strive to be a trained man and to inspire others to do the same."

Another great way for your mentees to learn that mentoring extends throughout one's lifetime is to introduce them to someone who is a mentor to you. You can simply go out for dinner and have the three of you talk about your individual relationships. Or you can take an even more direct approach and have your mentee come along when you seek advice from your mentor. For example, if you and your mentee are exploring possible careers the young person wants to pursue, you can turn to your mentor for help in making connections and looking at different options. To see a trusted guide seek counsel from an elder will be a wonderful inspiration for a young person.

"Linda had been my mentor for a couple of years," recalls Brent, who is studying design in New Orleans and who was mentored through a church-based program in his hometown of Baton Rouge. "We were really tight, you know. She helped me get focused on a career, get my act together in school. I looked to her for the straight talk, and she was always there for me and always honest.

"A couple of months into my senior year of high school, things got really bad at home for me. My mother had gotten together again with a man who had been in and out of our lives for the past six years, always bringing with him fear and violence. There were fights, all-night drinking binges, broken furniture—more and more chaos. Finally, I felt like I was at the end of my rope. I didn't know what to do, except that I knew I had to get out of that house.

"I went to see Linda. I'd been telling her some of what had been going on, but now I laid it all out and asked for her help. She looked at me very seriously for a few moments and said, 'Brent, I think on this one we both need help. I am not sure how to advise you, but I do have someone who will know what to do. Her name is Dorothy. She is a retired federal judge, and she has been my mentor for nearly a decade.'

"Linda had never mentioned that she had a mentor, so I was a little surprised. But I was also pleased. It seemed right that Linda would have someone who helped her out.

"We went to see Dorothy together a day or so afterward. She lived in a neat house—a place that looked like it had been designed for thinking and comfort—in one of the quieter neighborhoods. She served us mint iced tea in the parlor, and we chitchatted for a few minutes about the weather and the upcoming holidays.

"The small talk did not last long, though. Dorothy looked at Linda and said, 'You said on the phone that you wanted to get my advice about something. What is it?' Linda laughed and replied, 'Oh, Dorothy, I can always count on you to get to the heart of things. Thank you.' Then she took a breath and laid out the situation in a few precise, carefully thought-out sentences.

"Dorothy listened intently and shook her head with a look of recognition and regret. 'I am sorry that you are going through that, Brent,' she said when Linda finished. 'Well now, let's see what the options are.' And with that she began to go through various scenarios of how I could deal with the problem.

"The three of us spent the better part of two hours weighing different alternatives. Finally, we agreed that my best bet was to try to declare myself an emancipated minor and to leave the house. I was a few months short of my eighteenth birthday, had a good part-time job at a department store, and had family nearby with whom I could stay until I went off to college. My chances of making it on my own were quite good, and the court would be likely to take that into account and grant my petition.

"Dorothy explained to Linda and me the procedures for filing a petition, ways to expedite the process, and things to watch out for. She then gave us the name of an acquaintance who worked at a local youth-advocacy organization that handled cases like mine.

"It was an amazing feeling to have this woman whom I had never met before take so much time to help me deal with my problems. And it was really cool to see the mutual respect and warmth that Linda and Dorothy had for each other. It was this no-nonsense kind of affection, the kind you know you can count on no matter what. I knew, right there and then, that I wanted to have relationships like that as I went through my own life."

Mentoring Young Mentors

As we witness the past decade and move into the new millennium, we see a great deficit of mentors available to guide our young people. To address this problem, we at the 100 Black Men of America established the Collegiate 100, which trains college students to be mentors to high school students.

The 100 sees the Collegiate 100 as a gold mine to furthering the number of mentors, because these young people are not far away from their own experience of being mentored and are in touch with the issues of growing up in today's society. This program also gives college students a way to stay connected to their community and sensitizes them to the importance of seeking out mentors after they graduate college and move up the professional ladder.

The Gallup Organization study of the 100 Black Men of America, Inc., mentoring programs showed that 87 percent of the 800 participants had someone they considered as a mentor while growing up. It is not at all surprising that people who had mentors tend to become mentors themselves. When someone gives you such a gift, the best way to show your gratitude is to give to others.

"I am going to be a mentee my whole life," says Dijuan S. Kellom, a mentee at the Atlanta chapter of the 100 Black Men of America, Inc., who is a freshman at Morehouse College and the executive director of the Collegiate 100. "There will always be someone I will look to for guidance and advice. You never stop growing as long as you keep looking for people to learn from.

"I am now a mentor to others because I know how much it helped me to have someone to guide me. It is very fulfilling to be able to give back. It is especially nice to see the effect you have on a kid's life, when you help him grow and change and alter his mindset. And I learn, also. That's the great thing.

"Through the Collegiate 100, we take mentoring to the next level. We've got college students from all around Atlanta who are mentored by members of the 100 Black Men of Atlanta. They, in turn, mentor one hundred fifty kids from the sixth to the ninth grades in an academic program called Project Success.

"The cool thing about this is that Project Success was the first mentoring program of the 100 in Atlanta. They started out with one class and created a real blueprint for academic mentoring. We at the Collegiate 100 are the second generation, the younger brothers and sisters. And it's a wonderful feeling to step into that responsibility knowing that you've got someone to mentor you through the process."

Twenty-five-year-old Jamal Miller of Atlanta is another wonderful example of a mentee being part of the continuum of mentoring. "Now that I am mentoring young people, I understand that special feeling of lending a hand to a young person. I feel that I am giving back and representing the men who mentored me. It makes me feel so good to know that they would be proud of me. This sense of gratification about fulfilling your mentor's expectations of you, it feels like floating on cloud nine."

Encouraging your mentees to mentor others is not only a way to bring them into the circle but also a powerful way to demonstrate your trust and confidence and to build the youths' sense of competence and self-esteem. The best way to accomplish this is to help the boy or girl you are working with find a volunteer program that matches with his or her interests and brings together young people of different ages. Even though you will be available to guide your mentee, a structured environment is likely to make for a better first mentoring experience.

At the 100 Black Men of America, Inc., many of our chapters have active programs that bring college and high school students together. With the 100 New Stars Program, which is being tested in New York, Atlanta, and the Northern California Bay Area, we are extending youth-to-youth mentoring into elementary schools. Older youth and peers have a tremendous influence on children. And the way we see it, you are never too young to be mentored or to begin to reach out to others.

"In its first year, our 100 New Stars Program has been very successful," explains Mark E. Fant, chair of the mentoring committee of the One Hundred Black Men, Inc., in New York City. "Our members work with 104 student volunteers from the High School for Law, Government, and Justice in the Bronx. These students are mentored and trained to become mentors themselves. They then go into elementary schools in the Bronx and tutor younger children.

"The high school students get academic credit and letters of recommendation to use for college and work applications. The students really like the program because it puts a different spin on their education. They get to learn some really significant life skills and to learn, at an early age, how to work with younger people in a productive, supportive way. And the elementary school kids love having these cool older kids take the time to help them with their reading and math. To them, it's like having their older siblings let them tag along to a game or a party. It's acceptance, and a helping hand, and someone to look up to.

"We are now working with the New York City Board of Education to expand the program to other schools. We want to see as many kids as possible get involved and benefit from having a mentor and being mentors at the same time."

The idea of youth mentoring youth is a very powerful one. And there are many ways to bring young people into the circle of mentoring as mentors. We at the 100 are reaching out to other organizations to help them start youth-to-youth mentoring programs using the Collegiate 100 as a model. You also may want to start a program in your community if there is not one available. In fact, that might be a great project for you and your mentee to work on together.

"When I was playing professional football," says Bruce Harper, the former MVP running back with the New York Jets, "I would go to schools and talk to kids. I loved doing that. It always brought a big smile to my face to know I was making a real difference off the field. It's a great responsibility to work with young people, but it made me proud and filled my heart to see how I could affect another human being.

"When I stopped playing professionally, I joined Athletes Helping Athletes, a mentoring group on Long Island. That was a really great experience. In 1998, I started my own organization in New Jersey patterned on this group.

"Heroes and Cool Kids is a not-for-profit organization that connects professional athletes and high-profile amateur athletes with high school athletes. The purpose is to train the young people—most of whom are in the tenth and eleventh grades—to be mentors to fifth- and sixth-grade students.

"The professional athletes—we've got everyone involved, men, women, black, white, Latino—train the high school students and give inspirational examples from their sports experiences. They impart lessons they have learned through playing sports to motivate and inform the students.

"We then have the students visit the elementary schools, one boy and one girl per classroom. The first visit is to get acquainted; the second deals with sportsmanship; and the third with preventing substance abuse.

"This is our first year and we are working with approximately seventy-five high school athletes from three schools. The students are selected by their athletic department, coaches, and physical education teachers. We hope to expand the program in the coming years. Our goal is to create a dialogue between kids and to bring the lessons of sports off the fields and into the classroom."

Mentoring for a Lifetime

Transitions are often the most difficult times in our lives. That is especially true for young people, for whom the movement from adolescence to early adulthood is a time of great upheaval, constant change, and tremendous uncertainty. You, as a mentor, serve as an anchor, a steadying, reassuring presence in your mentee's life. It stands to reason that the idea of the relationship, as you have known it, coming to an end might fill your mentee with a sense of apprehension and loss. Needless to say, you too are likely to feel sad at the prospect of letting go of someone who has come to play an important part in your life. The end of a formal mentoring relationship, however, is an essential part of your mentee's development.

This transition is an opportunity to teach your mentee how to deal with feelings that come with major life changes. It is also a chance to reinforce the idea that we all need mentors throughout our lives and to help the young person develop the skills of finding people willing to offer that kind of support.

There is no prescribed length of time a mentoring relationship should last. Many span one to four years. Others are longer; a few are shorter. It really depends on how old your mentee is when you start and whether the goals you set for the relationship are met. A good many mentoring relationships end when the young person graduates from high school and goes to college or gets a job. The important thing is to watch for the beginning of the transition—the subtle movement of the young person toward a more adult autonomy—and to end the relationship in a loving, conscious, productive way.

"I had been Rafael's mentor since he was in junior high school," recalls Juan, a computer software designer from Miami who mentors through a local mentoring partnership. "It took us a while to get to see eye to eye. I am Cuban, and Rafie is Dominican. So we had some stereotypes to get over before we could really start to bond. What really helped was our love of the water. For the first six or seven months, we did almost nothing but go out on my sailboat or fish or swim. We just hung, you know. No pressure. If things were going to work out, they would. And if not, well . . . maybe we weren't the right match.

"But water has a way of getting into your heart. And as we spent time together, the conversation began to flow. I told Rafie stories about growing up on Calle Ocho in the late seventies. He talked about visiting his father in the Dominican Republic and, with time, even about how angry he was about his parents' divorce.

"As we got closer and there was more trust, we began to do more structured things. I brought him to my office, took him along on press checks at the printers, taught him how to use computer graphics programs. We talked about school and his interest in different subjects. I met with his teachers and helped find tutors to improve Rafie's performance in English and math.

"It was a good time. We were really accomplishing a lot and developing a strong bond. One day, it was about a week before my birthday in November, Rafie called at the office and asked if he could stop by to give me something. I said, of course he could, and waited with curiosity. He showed up in an hour, still with his schoolbag on his shoulder, and grinning in a shy kind of way, gave me an intricately carved wooden Neptune.

" 'Happy birthday,' he said. 'Rafie, this is beautiful. Where did you get it?' I asked. 'I made it,' he replied. 'What do you mean you made it? I've known you for a year and a half, and you never said anything about carving or sculpting,' I said incredulously. 'Oh, it's no big deal. My grandfather taught me how to do it. I just fool around.'

"I wasn't about to let it go at that. The kid obviously had real talent. But he was awfully shy about it. Over the next few weeks, we talked and talked about it. I asked Rafie to show me his other carvings, and there were a good many pieces that looked like the work of an accomplished craftsman. I knew that there was great untapped potential in him, and I wanted to help him become the artist he promised to be.

"I encouraged Rafie to take art classes, to develop his technique, to experiment with other media. And I could see him listening to me. He enrolled in a still-life drawing class. We started going to museums together. He okayed my idea of sending away for catalogs for him from the Rhode Island School of Design and the New York Studio School.

"But finally, though, he had enough. 'I've got a confession to make, Juan,' he said to me on one of our outings to a local gallery. 'What I'm really interested in is making furniture.'

"I was taken aback. 'You mean like carved stuff—sort of art pieces?' 'No,' he said in a clear-eyed sort of way, 'I mean furniture. Like tables and chairs and shelves. Carving figures is something I do for myself. It's private, you know. I don't want to make it into a job. I just want to keep it for me and the people I care about. But I would like to make beautiful things that people can use in their houses—things they will love and pass down to their kids.'

"Well, what could I say to that? Rafie knew what he wanted, and although I found it difficult to understand, I trusted him enough to know that he had thought about what he said very carefully. 'Okay,' I answered, 'let's find out where you can learn about furniture design.

"With that, we began to research the options that were available to Rafie. There were academic programs, trade schools, and apprenticeships. We wrote away for catalogs, spoke to people on the phone, discussed the various alternatives. But even as we were doing all of these things together, I sensed that Rafie was looking beyond our relationship. It sort of felt to me like he kept searching the horizon for something I could not even see.

"It was a strange feeling to have invested so much of myself into helping this kid grow and now to see him getting ready to strike out on his own. It was this powerful mixture of grief, pride, confidence, and hope. I knew that a part of our relationship was coming to an end and that I needed to find a way to help Rafie make the transition smoothly.

"Finally, I figured that I needed him to tell me what it was that he was looking for. 'I've been afraid to say this to you,' he said, looking at me with a slight frown, 'because I thought you would be disappointed. But what I really want right now is to get a job at one of those fine furniture makers in North Carolina. Maybe I'll want to go to college later for the design stuff. But for right now, I want to get my hands on the wood and the tools—I want to see my pieces get loaded on trucks and shipped out to showrooms around the country.'

"Again, Rafie had been able to think through and articulate the direction he wanted his life to take. I wasn't about to try to dissuade him. On the other hand, I did not really feel equipped to help him achieve his goal. I felt like my job was over, except for one last thing. I really wanted to teach Rafie how to find other people along the way who would help him figure things out, who would look out for him.

"As we worked on his application letters together, I began to tell him about the concept of apprenticeship, of established craftspeople training and mentoring young people just starting out. 'Look for the ones who are willing to give you a hand,' I advised. 'The men and women who will take time out to show you how to get something done or to talk to you about your work. And when you identify them, don't be afraid just to walk up to them and ask if they would be willing to be your mentors. Being open to receiving guidance and support is the key to finding people who will give them to you. Developing the confidence to ask for help is a skill that will serve you the rest of your life.'

"In a few months, after an extensive job search, Rafie was offered positions by two highly regarded furniture makers. He took the one that offered a formal mentoring program for new employees. Eventually, he told me before he left Miami, he is contemplating going back to school and designing his own furniture line."

Mentoring in Your Professional Life

We all need mentors in our careers as well as in our personal lives. There is a certain loneliness and alienation that every one of us experiences as we pursue our careers, and this feeling is especially acute in Corporate America. The concept of acting as a mentor in a work situation is the same as mentoring a young person: it is taking the time to share your experiences with others, guiding them along the way, and, ultimately, making a difference in their future.

According to a recent study of minority women in business conducted by the Catalyst organization, the lack of a mentor was cited as the number one barrier to progress. Many of the 1,700 managers and professionals interviewed said that social barriers and the chance to network informally with colleagues was keeping them from advancing and cracking the "glass or concrete ceiling," despite diversity programs in their companies.

Mentoring takes place all along the road, even when you are just beginning your career. As a mentor in the professional world, you:

- Serve as a visible role model, a nonjudgmental counselor, and a trusted sounding board while acting as a buffer and guide.
- Bring the talents of your mentee to the attention of people of power and provide access to crucial professional networks.
- Make the difference between isolation and invisibility and professional recognition and growth.

Bill Campbell, Mayor of Atlanta, once described mentoring as grafting yourself onto the life of a young person who is searching for direction. That is a wonderful image, with all its connotations of nurturing and tending. But it is not just yourself that you graft onto the young person, it is also all of the people who mentored you, and the ones who mentored them, in turn.

Having had the opportunity to be mentored, and now having the responsibility of being a mentor, I think of myself as planting seeds of trees whose fruit I may never see. I firmly believe that I must continue to plant these seeds out of a sense of responsibility and out of a desire to pass the torch to the next generation.

Like the individuals who did battle during the Civil Rights movement in this country, we must not give up. If we don't continue to mentor from generation to generation, this country cannot remain strong and prosperous into the next millennium. If the cycle is broken, hope will be lost.

Simply by giving your time and attention to a young person, you pass on the values of social responsibility, communal action, and empathy. Mentoring is a powerful connection between generations, a way to preserve our tradition of "passing on." As a mentor, you are as strengthened and enriched as the person you are mentoring. Remember, to keep the dream alive, many others must pass through the door and join you. It is up to you to make sure that door is open for those who follow.

What You Can Do:

1. Find a mentor[s] for yourself.
2. Teach your mentee how to seek out mentors throughout his or her lifetime.
3. Pass on your passion for mentoring to a young person.

CHAPTER SEVEN

Partnerships for the Future: Collaborating for Success

Community cannot feed for long on itself, it can only flourish with the coming of others from beyond, their unknown and undiscovered brothers.

—HOWARD THURMAN

As your commitment to mentoring young people becomes deeper with experience, you may want to think about expanding the mentoring community in your area by reaching out to local organizations, educational institutions, government agencies, and corporations to build partnerships dedicated to helping youth develop and grow. If you mentor through an existing program, you can see if you can get your employer or union or fraternal organization to get involved with the program. If there is no formal program where you live, see whether you can bring people together from such places as the school board, local college, or community organizations to start a mentoring partnership. The possibilities are endless.

Now, I am not saying it's easy to pull folks together. It takes vision, perseverance, and patience. On the other hand, getting together in support of kids is an idea that is easy for people to get excited about. It makes sense from a personal, social, and corporate perspective. The point is to demonstrate to the people you are trying to bring together the potential for, to use an old expression, "doing well by doing good."

In the nearly 16 years that I worked with U.S. Senator Sam Nunn—one of my greatest mentors—on Capitol Hill and in Georgia, I learned the strategic way of going about getting things done. I learned that people could disagree with each other and still work together, that a strong ally one day can be a powerful critic the next, and that losing a battle does not mean you have lost the war. Commitment and knowing how to compromise are everything.

Out of my experience, I have distilled the following eight principles for achieving one's goals:

1. Have a plan.
2. Never promise more than you can deliver.
3. Do not try to be all things to all people.
4. Communicate what you are trying to do on a one-to-one level and to the community at large.

5. Find friends to support you and your objective.
6. Build coalitions.
7. Concede small points in order to accomplish the larger goal.
8. Believe in what you are doing and stay focused.

These principles have served me well in realizing my personal vision and in my work with the 100 Black Men of America, Inc. In the course of building our mentoring programs, we have seen that most communities are committed to addressing the needs of their children and are very creative in securing resources and finding dedicated volunteers and partners for productive collaborations.

"Promise of Progress" is an innovative program created by the Phoenix chapter of the 100 to involve college students in mentoring. It involves a partnership with the University of Arizona that brings students into the circle of mentoring by encouraging them to mentor younger people in the city schools.

"My mother and I moved to Phoenix from Detroit when I was thirteen," says Isaiah, now a sophomore at the University of Arizona who mentors through the "Promise of Progress" program. "It was a really hard time. I didn't know anybody. I started hanging out with the street gang in my neighborhood, getting into trouble. I still have my tattoo to remind me how close I came to throwing my life away.

"I got lucky, though. The 100 was working with my school, and I was assigned to a group of tough kids who were being mentored. It was like somebody threw me a lifeline. I suddenly had all these men to look up to and other kids who were struggling with the same stuff I was.

"Your mindset can only change if you are exposed to different ways of handling things. And here were these successful black men who were saying, 'Look, there is a different path, a different light to see by.' They did not owe me anything. They did not have to be there. They were doing it because they cared, because they wanted to give back.

"That has been my model for how I want to be. It is not enough to succeed. You have to share the success, or it does not mean anything. So, that is why I mentor, because I know how much I got out of being mentored and I want to pay back.

In his freshman year of college, Isaiah began tutoring middle school students in math and science and helping them with their homework. Then he started doing college entrance test preparation.

"It was amazing to see these tough guys getting all excited about figuring out how to solve a geometry problem," he marvels. "It's even more fantastic when one of them comes up to you in the hallway and says, 'I got trouble. Can you help?'

"That was the thing I was not prepared for. I have these school kids looking up to me, asking me for advice on how to handle things. When that happens, you have to take a different look at yourself. I have to walk the walk, you know. If I mess up, it is not just me I am disappointing. How am I going to explain it to these guys? It's a gift, this responsibility. I say it's a gift because it makes me proud to know that I'm living up to it."

Herbert W. Jackson, president of the Phoenix chapter, who is a labor-relations attorney and national secretary of the 100 Black Men of America, adds: "Mentors do not want or need public acknowledgment. Just knowing you have touched people is enough. African Americans make up less than four percent of the population of Phoenix. As a result, our members are important role models for the young African Americans who live here and we are aware of our responsibility to them. We also sponsor a Mentoring Education Network (MEN) for older high school students, in which they learn about becoming responsible fathers and husbands, in addition to pursuing fulfilling careers.

"Our chapter provides its members with a variety of mentoring options—one-on-one, group, older kids, younger kids. As long as you are mentoring, you are doing service to your community."

Shirley Chisholm has said, "Service is the rent you pay for room on this earth." This is one of the central lessons of all the mentoring programs of the 100 Black Men of America. In order to succeed in our mission of helping to create a legacy of hope for our community, we cannot be satisfied with opening doors for just one generation. The purpose of programs such as "Promise of Progress" ensures that each successive generation sees itself as responsible for those who follow after them.

In the coming pages, you will read about some of the partnerships the 100 and its chapters have formed to ensure that communities throughout the country provide effective mentoring programs that care about young people and their futures, encourage youth to aspire to reach their full potential, and support all children as they strive to formulate and work toward visions of their own lives. I hope that these examples of successful alliances will be an inspiration to you as you begin to think about building a mentoring community of your own.

Educational Institutions

"I was a problem child growing up," says Rudy Coombs, a supervisor with the U.S. Postal Service and a member of the One Hundred Black Men, Inc., in New York City. "I can relate to kids who don't have advantages handed to them, who have to struggle. That is why I take time out to mentor. I can communicate to young people, and they listen and relate to me.

"I graduated from Theodore Roosevelt High School in the Bronx in 1971 and went to Paine College in Augusta, Georgia. But I always knew that I would come back to New York, and when I did, I headed straight for my old school to see how I could volunteer my time. The student population of Roosevelt had increased to four thousand, most of whom were from economically disadvantaged minority families. I wanted to do something, to give back.

"I started out as a motivational speaker. I talked to the students myself, and I brought in business people, nurses, lawyers—all kinds of professionals—to introduce the kids to different role models. In 1996, I began working with the One Hundred Black Men to have the organization officially adopt the school. Thelma Baxter, the principal—she is the first African American principal at the school—was really instrumental in helping us get started and has been totally supportive every step of the way.

"Our mentoring programs are quite diverse. We offer the students one-on-one mentoring in partnership with Big Brothers/Big Sisters. We also do group mentoring and a slew of academic programs, such as tutoring and college entrance examination preparation. We've even raised money to buy 144 computers for the school.

"It is very gratifying to see the program I started become so successful. But it is the one-on-one contact that keeps me coming back. I have two mentees right now: Nicole, who will be attending Hampton College next year, and Jamal, who will study at Baruch College. I see them graduate and go off to college, and it is an awesome feeling. When they come back to me and tell me what they're doing and how I affected them—that I reached them—that's what life is all about. Nothing else in the world can make you feel that good."

Schools are a natural partner for mentoring programs. You can start with one school and offer to bring in adults to mentor the students. Or if you have more resources, you can take on a district or even the whole local school board. The important thing is not to overreach: Keep in mind that the politics of education can be quite complex. You will need to build a strong coalition with support from parents, the community, local business, and appropriate government bodies. Keep your focus and remember that when you succeed, it will be the children in your community who will benefit.

"All of our mentoring programs are conducted in close cooperation with the New York City Board of Education," explains Mark E. Fant, chair of the mentoring committee of the One Hundred Black Men in New York City. "We have one-on-one mentoring, group mentoring, and scholarships and tutorial programs that include between two thousand and three thousand young men and women throughout the city. We work through the guidance offices in the schools where the kids fill out applications for a mentor. They are then selected on the basis of their commitment to community service, their grades, and their aspirations for the future. Because each of our mentees gets a scholarship, our screening process is very thorough. We also work very closely with parents—we consider this a joint venture.

"The scholarship program is supported by corporate sponsors, who adopt a class for four years. Each recipient gets a scholarship of between $4,000 and $6,000. And we hold these young people accountable by having ongoing follow-ups during the course of their four years at college. Our slogan is: 'Staying the Course.'

"Every one of the fourteen students we gave scholarships to in 1995 graduated from college in 1999—from such schools as Cornell University, Princeton University, Amherst College, Oberlin College, and Virginia Union University. These are accomplishments that all of us are really proud of."

"The scholarship program is a pipeline of excellence," adds Norman J. McCullough, deputy director of the Department of Equal Opportunity at the New York City Housing Authority and chair of the education committee of the New York chapter of the 100. "It was started in 1981, under the guidance of Dr. Roscoe Brown, the well-known educator and past president of the One Hundred Black Men, Inc.

"At that time, we had four students; in 1999, we have seventeen scholarship recipients going to such colleges as Morehouse College, Cornell University, Brown University, and Sophie Davis Medical School of the City University of New York. At any given time, we have more than sixty students in our scholarship program.

"We also have an SAT Prep Program in collaboration with the Princeton Review. We hire teachers to prepare juniors and seniors in high school—who are also recommended to us by their guidance counselors—to take the test. Currently, there are one hundred students in the program."

Institutions of higher education—any institutions of learning, really—are important members of a mentoring community because of their capacity to expand young people's minds and broaden their horizons. Colleges and universities can play pivotal roles as mentoring partners. Programs such as the Collegiate 100 in Atlanta and Promise of Progress in Phoenix, both of which involve college students as mentors and tutors to high school students, are good examples of such partnerships. Our Detroit chapter's Early Identification Program, which works with the University of Michigan at Dearborn to help high school students with low grade-point averages improve their performance and get into college, is another example of a productive educational collaboration.

Youth-Serving Organizations

"In Chicago, we believe that quality is more important than quantity," says Harry L. Coaxum, board chair of the 100 Black Men of Chicago. "We work with sixty young men, between eleven and eighteen years of age. We hold weekly sessions at the Michele Clark Middle School and South Carolina Community Services. There is one-on-one mentoring of at-risk youth from the inner city, counseling, tutoring, and educational field trips.

"We also have a Y-Pal Program through a local YMCA. The sessions vary. Sometimes they are formally structured, and other times they are more freewheeling, allowing the kids to discuss what is on their minds. In addition, the chapter has SAT and ACT preparation programs.

"We put a great deal of emphasis on partnerships. In coming together with other organizations, there is the excitement of sharing the synergy of common purpose, of working for something we all believe in.

"These programs help the young people on an individual basis but also society as a whole. When you see young kids feeling good about themselves and becoming more self-reliant, you know you're on to something. They see that you can have dreams and can aspire to achieve them. They learn that there are people who care and are willing to work to help them reach their dreams.

"There is value in what we're doing. We help young people get through the 'glass walls' in this country—the barriers between racial, religious, and cultural groups. We need to break down these walls and show that there are more similarities than differences.

"Mentoring is a real-life example of people coming together for the greater good. Jackie Robinson's tombstone says: 'The measure of a man's life is the impact he has on the people around him.' Well, your impact has to go beyond immediate family and friends. As a mentor, you get to pass the baton, to shape and influence another human being. It doesn't get a whole lot better than that."

Local youth-serving organizations, community centers, and other social-service agencies are also important potential partners in building a mentoring community. Chapters of national organizations such as the YMCA, the YWCA, Big Brothers/Big Sisters, Boy and Girl Scouts, to name a few, as well as many local nonprofit and neighborhood centers, have trained staff who work with young people, facilities, and even existing programs that can be integrated into mentoring. For instance, the Cleveland chapter of the 100 Black Men of America works with the local Boys Town, an organization that helps young men who have been removed from their homes. Members of the 100 offer group mentoring to 20 youths—ages 11 to 19—as well as one-on-one mentoring through the school at Boys Town.

Another excellent example of a successful local mentoring partnership is the computer literacy initiative of the Metro St. Louis chapter of the 100. Thomas R. Bailey, Jr., former president of the chapter, explains: "This was the brainchild of Marvin Johnson, a member who is a computer consultant with Maryville Technologies. Marvin arranged for the first computers to be donated and got the whole thing off the ground. The kids' reaction has been fantastic."

Marvin Johnson elaborates: "I grew up in the projects of Nashville, Arkansas. No one in my immediate community had any knowledge of math above algebra, let alone an understanding of computers. So when I went to college, I didn't have the tools that other students had. I studied electrical engineering at the University of Arkansas in Fayetteville, and it was a real struggle to catch up in developing the kinds of computer skills I needed to succeed.

"Computer literacy is now crucial to getting a good education and making it in the work world. I don't want our kids to have to face the same problems I did. That has really been the inspiration for my work with the computer literacy program.

"When the idea first came up, we at the 100 decided to look for a location where kids were already being served. The Youth and Family Services Center, which is located in one of St. Louis's inner-city neighborhoods, was a perfect partner for us. With a whole range of after-school activities, it attracts boys and girls ages five through eighteen. It's a place where kids feel welcomed and appreciated.

"We started the program in 1998. Several local companies donated about one hundred fifty computers, and we brought in the St. Louis Community College as the third partner to provide instructors and student interns. The 100 pays the instructors' salaries, and the interns get college credit for their work.

"The program is open to kids as young as seven, as long as they can read, and goes up to age twelve. There are twelve computer stations, and eight to ten kids in each class. The program runs fifteen weeks and includes: an introduction to computers, with software donated from the United Way; a Microsoft Word class; and a math skills class.

"When they complete the program, the kids get a diploma signed by St. Louis Community College, the 100 Black Men of Metro St. Louis, and the Youth and Family Services Center. The best part, though, is that they get a free computer, loaded with all the latest software. In return, they commit to coming back to the program to teach or help other kids.

"There has been a tremendous response from the students. So far, one hundred thirty students have graduated, and we will soon be entering into a second partnership with Carver Center to expand the program to include another two hundred to three hundred kids."

Brenda Jones, program director of the Youth and Family Services Center, underscores the importance of this program to the children in the community her organization serves: "You have to remember that many of these kids have been written off by the system and are in special education classes or in vocational training. For many of them, this program is the first opportunity to see that learning can be fun.

"The 100 Black Men brings to the program a knowledge of technology; business acumen; role models and mentors to interact with the students; help with funding; and an ongoing commitment. Marvin Johnson, in particular, has been a tireless friend of the program. He set up the whole network and continues to provide all the technical support.

"Without this kind of collaborative effort, we could not offer our children the learning opportunities they need to succeed. This summer we will run a computer camp that will provide intensive training over the course of three weeks. Graduates will receive a Microsoft A+ Certificate that indicates proficiency in operating hardware and software. These certificates are very useful in securing good employment."

Eleven-year-old Jamaica Eller, who graduated from the computer literacy program when she was nine and is now a tutor, puts it this way: "I couldn't believe it. I'd played on my mom's computer at work before, but now I am learning things like how to make my own note paper, how to draw and print pictures, how to use Microsoft Word, and best of all how the computer works. I actually know what goes on in there. That's just too cool."

Jamaica is right. Initiatives like this—ones that unite people around the common cause of helping our children aspire and achieve—are really cool. And all it takes to make them come to life is one person with vision and persistence.

The housing program of the 100 Black Men of Broward County, Florida, is a superb example of a cutting-edge economic development initiative that also serves as a mentoring experience for the young people of the community. The members of the chapter decided that the most important challenge facing their community was the lack of decent housing and so went about changing the situation by helping to create and build hundreds of affordable new homes in the Fort Lauderdale area.

"The best thing about this program is that our mentees have an opportunity to participate in reinvesting in their own community," says Andre Williams, president of the Broward County chapter. "Not only do they get a chance to be vocationally instructed in construction and restoration skills, they also learn about different career opportunities in such fields as banking, mortgage lending, and real estate.

"This is a creative form of mentoring because our young people can see for themselves that we are not just offering people homes. We are also creating jobs, stimulating the local economy, and rebuilding the community, which will hopefully lead to better schools, safer streets, and higher community expectations. By being involved, our kids are becoming invested in wanting to make a better future for themselves and their families.

"For example, we have two young men who want to be architects. They are always at the building sites talking to the designers or watching the builders. They are soaking in all this learning. Basking in it. And these are kids who were barely keeping up in school a couple of years ago. It's like what we always say: 'What they see is what they'll be.' But I tell you, it's great to see it happening right in front of your eyes.

"This initiative is making approximately four hundred homes available to the people of our community over the next three years. All of the houses will be equipped with computer systems, security alarms, security systems, sprinklers—the latest technology. They are valued from $68,900 to $96,000.

"The State of Florida ranks last in lending to minorities, so we have had to lead the way on this and throw all our resources at this problem. As a result, we contact and negotiate with our own mortgage lenders. We have also arranged for $15,000 grants from the city for first-time home buyers.

"One of the most emotional moments during the groundbreaking ceremony for our first house was seeing the faces of the kids and hearing them speak with such pride. They were suddenly saying, 'Wait a minute. We're part of this. We're somebody.' This was an amazing thing for them—the realization that they had weight in the world. For me, that is the ultimate reward. Whatever else these kids will go on to do in life, they have the knowledge that they made a difference in the lives of the people around them. I bet they are going to go on making a difference."

The Broward Chapter of the 100 also emphasizes computer training in its mentoring program and boasts its own computer center, which is open to the public. Young people take part in essay writing contests on their computers and are instructed in creating Web sites and Web pages, an extremely marketable skill in today's business world. In addition, the chapter is involved in a partnership with the Broward Performing Arts Center that allows the young people to attend certain events free of charge so they can be exposed to the theater, opera, ballet, and classical music.

"When I played football at Florida State University," Andre Williams says, "my coach Bobby Bowden shared this with me: 'Sooner or later life will end on the football field and you will have eighty percent of your life ahead.' I'm proud of my mentoring work because I'm helping these kids to be productive in society. The 100 teaches young people not just to say give me, give me, but to be independent and put something back into their community."

Unions, Associations, and Fraternal Organizations

We have spoken at length about the critical importance of role models to young people. Working with unions and professional associations—as well as such other organizations as fraternities and alumnae groups—is a wonderful way to bring in many people who can serve as role models in your mentoring community. To look at how such a partnership works, let's return to the Aviation Camp run by the 100 Black Men of Louisville that we heard about in Chapter Four.

"I flew fighters in the Marine Corps, and now I pilot jets for UPS," says Houston Mills, director of the Aviation Camp. "I'm also a member of the Organization of Black Airline Pilots (OBAP), comprised of seven hundred black pilots who fly commercial airplanes in the United States. Think about it, African Americans make up only one percent of all commercial pilots in this country!

"The idea behind the Aviation Camp, which has just completed its fifth year, was to expose young people in the metropolitan Louisville area to the world of aviation and to the career opportunities available in this exciting field. The key, of course, was getting the right people lined up to make it possible.

"Ultimately, a wonderful partnership coalesced around the idea. It includes the 100 Black Men of Louisville, UPS, OBAP, and Shawnee High School, a magnet school for those interested in aviation careers. Each of us pitches in to provide a truly unique and enriching experience for the kids.

"This is how it works. Members of the 100 work with four or five African American volunteers from OBAP to run the camp that is held at Shawnee High School. For one week during the summer, about fifty kids—mostly black, disadvantaged, middle-school boys and girls—attend classes on aviation skills, history of black aviators and astronauts, communications, and team building techniques. We also have daily exploratory field trips.

"The students get a chance to pilot a state-of-the-art 757 flight simulator located at UPS headquarters. They also go for a short spin in a single-engine Cessna where they can see the controls of the plane close up. For many young people, it's their first time on an airplane. Even though some of them are afraid, they are all filled with wonder and awe. It makes me feel so good to see them enjoy the beauty of flying.

"The best part of the summer is the final trip. We fly the kids on a field trip to some important place in aviation history. UPS provides a 747 and we have an All-African-American crew. Last year, we went to the Kennedy Space Center in Florida where we got a personal tour from Robert Curbeeng, the black astronaut. The kids were totally blown away, to put it mildly.

"We've also gone to the Smithsonian Institution in Washington, D.C. On that trip, we had fifty kids on the flight, along with parents and chaperones. At the Smithsonian, we were greeted by General Earl Brown, the veteran black fighter pilot, and numerous members of the local chapter of the Tuskegee Airmen. These distinguished men then led the kids through an exhibit that highlighted the role that African Americans played in shaping modern aviation. It was really moving to see the instant bond that formed between the veterans and the young people. There was so much pride, respect, and hope. I am going to keep that memory with me for a long, long time."

Andrew Gazway, a seventh-grader who took part in the camp, summed up his experience this way: "Ever since I was a young boy, I've always wanted to fly. This camp exposed me to so much. I couldn't think of a better way to spend my vacation."

Like Andrew, most young people want to fly, in one way or another. Mentoring partnerships like the one between UPS, OBAP, Shawnee High School, and the 100 Black Men of Louisville make it possible for our children to soar.

Corporations

"There are certain things that corporations do because it's expected of us," says Dennis Malamatinas, CEO of Burger King Corporation. "Yet, for me personally, mentoring is something we do because I so strongly believe in it.

"At Burger King, we have BK Cares, our formal volunteering program for employees. BK Cares allows corporate employees to take up to two hours out of their work week to perform volunteer work within the community.

"Mentoring is easy and effective. The beauty of it is that it's about giving back. Young people need guidance, love, and role models. That's what mentoring—both formal and informal—provides for them.

"I came to this country when I was seventeen. I went through some tough times, so now, whenever I have the opportunity to help young people and offer them a hand, I do it. I know from my own experiences how important it is that someone reaches out to you and gives you a chance.

"Corporations are responsible to society and its citizens, and it's our obligation to set a role model for the community. Also, it is to our benefit to create a better world for tomorrow. Mentoring is a good and smart business solution. Why wouldn't you want a hand in helping to shape the next generation of our country? When we mentor, we are helping develop our future leaders, employees, and consumers.

"But nobody can do this alone. Collaborations between corporations and their noncorporate partners are working. Organizations like the 100 are the ones that are stirring things up and showing how we in the corporate world can be of help."

The times when corporations looked at nonprofit organizations as "charities" to which they donated money or products are coming to an end. "Indeed, a new paradigm for innovation is emerging," writes Harvard Professor Rosabeth Moss Kanter in the *Harvard Business Review.* "It is that the partnership between private enterprise and public interest produces profitable and sustainable change for both sides."

There are now tremendous opportunities to get businesses involved in your mentoring efforts. Many corporations are looking for ways to have their employees participate in the communities they serve. Therefore, companies are excellent sources of volunteers, facilities, internships, and other invaluable resources.

"Allstate started in Chicago in 1931, as part of Sears Roebuck," explains Andre Howell, director of corporate relations for Allstate Insurance, Co., who is a member of the Chicago chapter of the 100. "From the beginning, we have had a strong commitment to urban areas. And we continue to see them as valuable markets; they are our future.

"In my position, I create strategic relationships with other organizations. We place a special emphasis on urban institutions. These days, corporations have less money for philanthropy so we give in different ways. For instance, fifty-four percent of Allstate's fifty-five thousand employees do some kind of volunteer work.

"We are especially interested in mentoring, because the young people we are working with are going to be our customers and employees someday. We want to help shape their futures. Formal mentoring speaks to the importance of adult role models in young people's lives.

"But mentoring has to be done right. It is not a revolving door. You need commitment to giving back from the heart. That is why we do a lot of partnerships with the 100. In addition to the background checks and screenings that they do, they have established criteria that ensure quality mentoring: consistency, solid training, and continuity. For us in corporate America, it is important to have partners who bring that kind of business savvy to serving our communities."

Corporations are looking for partners who understand their strategic goals and are willing to collaborate on creating programs that advance these objectives while contributing to creating real social change. When you look to involve business in your mentoring community, begin by asking the question, "How is this going to allow the company to accomplish what it needs to do?" In answering that question together with the people from the corporation, you will establish the foundation for a productive and lasting alliance.

"One of the key goals of the 100 is to be accountable to the corporations and other partners whom we work with," says Herman Miller, vice president of our Silicon

Valley, California, chapter and national chair of our technology committee. "We are dedicated to employing the latest information technology and building a state-of-the-art infrastructure which will benefit all aspects of our management and productivity."

A senior manager at Sun Microsystems, Herman Miller believes that those nonprofit organizations that are fiscally responsible and technologically up-to-date are the ones viewed favorably when corporations look to create financial partnerships with community associations. As a result, the 100 Black Men of America now has a server-donated Web site that connects all chapters; a computer system in the national office that connects to every chapter; and staff in the national office dedicated solely to technology.

"Our information system gives us the capability to evaluate the progress of the participants in our various mentoring programs," he explains. "Eventually we hope to create a national database where we can follow our mentees as they get older and follow how they develop."

Corporations look for consistency and follow-through in their collaborations. "I have a motto, 'I inspect what I expect,' " says Willie Gregory, director, U.S. Business/Community Relations for Nike. "The 100 provides accountability, which is very important to us. Nike has contributed more than three million dollars to the 100's Miracle of Mentoring program over the past three years and the organization's tracking system allows us to see exactly how our money is being spent. In addition, since the funds are distributed to the local chapters, we know our involvement is having a direct impact on young people and not just being used for administrative costs. There is a human story behind each dollar we give.

"Even so, corporate involvement in the community is

not just about money. The consensus around Nike is that in order for a company to be a responsible member of society, it must invest in all aspects of a young person's life. So in addition to financial support, we also bring our corporate resources into our partnerships. For example, we use our contact with athletes to involve them in the mentoring programs. Athletes are natural role models for kids, and they emphasize the importance of staying focused on your goals. They also show young people how they in turn can mentor other kids.

"Partnering with nonprofit organizations and community groups is a win-win situation for us. For example, the 100 helps us to identify young people for internships at Nike and for eventual employment here. In this way, they are a part of developing and shaping the future of our company.

"Through mentoring collaborations, we get the opportunity to touch kids' lives. We help them grow into good citizens and good people. It is a reinvestment from what we get from our consumers. And what better place to put our money than into helping kids?

"As a corporation, we recognize that we cannot work in isolation. To touch all our kids, we need to work together. In the same way we study our financial portfolio when we plan our retirement, we should also look at how we treat young people because they are the most important part of our future.

"Ultimately, I believe it comes down to personal experience for all of us—we realize the importance of giving back. I am originally from Memphis, raised by my mother. My mentors came from my church, my high school, and my community. Since I was old enough to walk, the chair of the finance committee of our church was my mentor. He would tell me over and over that one day I would follow his lead. This was unstructured mentoring, but it sure produced dividends. He believed in me, and he was right. I am now the chair of the finance committee of our church—as he predicted—and following proudly in his footsteps!"

The 100 is fortunate to have so many great partners and corporate friends at its side as we attempt to serve the needs of the young, the future leaders of this world. Our partnerships rest on the mutual understanding that investing in youth reaps great benefits to all. And resources are not just financial. Our partners make available to us highly trained employees who volunteer in our mentoring programs, and they also offer internships and employment opportunities to our young people.

The companies we work with know that their commitment to the 100 is not a one-way street. They understand that the young people they help today are the employees, consumers, policy makers, and investors of tomorrow.

There is a saying: "One hundred years from now, nobody will care what kind of house I lived in or what kind of car I drove. What they will care about is what I did for our children." The sentiment within that statement is what brings all of us to mentoring. We feel the desire to give back to young people, to offer the kind of help that we got growing up, or we want to provide the kind of help we *didn't* get, but needed. Creating a community through creative coalitions and partnering involving the diverse sectors of our society is one of the most powerful ways to accomplish that goal.

What You Can Do:

1. Initiate mentoring programs in your workplace or community.
2. Use your personal and professional contacts to create mentoring partnerships.
3. Spread the word that investing in young people through mentoring is good corporate and public policy.

CHAPTER EIGHT

Being a Mentor: Now What?

Determination and perseverance move the world . . .

—MARVA COLLINS

Mentoring is an art. The relationship grows and matures, and you and your mentee grow with it. As you journey forward, you'll need to call on different abilities, and hone your understanding and your skills. In this chapter, we will review some of the basics of mentoring that you'll return to from time to time. As you mentor, use the following information as a touchstone, a reference, a means of ongoing support.

Keys to Successful Mentoring

Throughout this book, we have looked in depth at how to be a successful mentor. Whether you've become a mentor or are still thinking about it, here is a practical checklist of what it takes to make a real impact in a young person's life:

1. See your mentee regularly (once or twice a month—whatever you decide, make your commitment realistic).
2. Establish mutual trust.
3. Communicate regularly with your mentee's parents.
4. Help your mentee develop goals.
5. Help your mentee dress for success.
6. Be supportive and encourage your mentee.
7. Encourage your mentee to pursue the next level in education (e.g., high school, college, or postgraduate degree).
8. Talk with your mentee about what's right and wrong.
9. Develop a relationship in which the mentee is happy to see you when you get together.
10. Talk with your mentee to make sure he/she attends school every day.

11. Go to your mentee's school and community activities.
12. Help your mentee find a scholarship to fulfill his/her educational dream.
13. Illustrate and encourage the right behavior for certain situations.
14. With respect, correct your mentee when he or she misbehaves in any way.
15. Be supportive and encourage your mentee's interests.
16. Look for opportunities for you and your mentee to learn together.
17. Tell your mentee that you care about him or her and that his/her well-being is important.
18. Help your mentee understand why you cannot always be there for him or her.

As a mentor, you should aim to instill in a child a sense of self-confidence, competence, and cultural pride. Be consistent, committed, and caring, and you will profoundly affect the life of your mentee.

Suggested Activities

What you will want to do with your mentee will depend on the child's age and interests. However, here are a few suggestions to get you started.

- Take your mentee to your workplace and show him or her what you do for a living.

- Read a book.
- Visit an art or history museum.
- Go to the movies.
- Attend a sports event.
- Go hiking.
- Exercise.
- Attend a college fair.
- Surf the Web.
- Exchange e-mails.
- Visit a library.
- Make a budget to show your mentee how to manage money.
- Invite your mentee to a Sunday dinner, cookout, or other family activity at your home.
- Get involved in community action, like cleaning a park or repairing a playground.
- Help your mentee with schoolwork.
- Show your mentee how to write a résumé, cover letter, and thank-you note.
- Cook.
- Go to see your mentee's favorite musician perform at a concert.
- Attend a worship service.

No matter what you choose to do together, the real point is to create opportunities for conversation and learning. Mentoring is all about offering options and expanding horizons. So listen to your mentee, help him or her explore the world, be a supportive and encouraging force.

The Relationship with Your Mentee's Family

A mentor has to be sensitive to the mentee's parent(s) or guardian(s). You should never let your excitement about making a difference in a young person's life overshadow your responsibility to your mentee's family. A mentor's job is to enhance and stabilize the environment in which the child is growing up. You should never disrupt the balance in the family, usurp the parent's role, or strive to become the most important person in your mentee's life.

Communication is very important to ensuring that the mentee's family supports your relationship with their child. Talk with the young person's parent(s) or guardian(s). Explain your interest in mentoring and how the process of building the mentoring relationship works. Find out what the dreams and aspirations of the parents or guardians are for their child. As you help your mentee develop goals, make sure that the family understands and supports the direction the young person is heading in.

A mentor is not a parent. A mentor is a trusted friend and guide. Your purpose is not to provide your mentee with a surrogate family. Your role is to help expand the options available to the young person and to provide a new dimension to his or her relationship with adults.

Network of Support

One of the factors that makes the Miracles of Mentoring program so successful is the 100's emphasis on ongoing training and support for its mentors. We offer our volunteers a network—both through national and local meetings and on-line interaction—that gives them access to others who are also mentoring.

It is very important that you find a mentoring community, whether formal or informal, to make sure that you have the support you need. You may have questions, or you may face situations where you do not know what is best to do. By being connected to others, you will have a variety of resources to call upon.

Mentoring is a continuous process. You and your mentee learn by doing as the relationship unfolds. Don't be afraid to make mistakes. Don't be afraid to ask for help. The art of formal mentoring is constantly evolving, and it is part of your commitment to mentoring to stay current with the best practices in the field.

Once you mentor, you will always remain a mentor. You might take a break from formal mentoring, but remember that you are constantly serving as a role model to younger people, even if you aren't aware of it. The power to create miracles is within you, the only choice is how you use it.

What You Can Do:

1. Keep your mentoring skills up-to-date.
2. Be creative in your interactions with your mentee.
3. Create a mentoring group or team, made up of other mentors. Propose to meet once a month to exchange ideas about mentoring. (This can also be done on-line.)
4. Stay in touch with other mentors.

CHAPTER NINE

Each One, Reach One, Teach One: An Act of Faith in the Circle of Life

And when we allow freedom to ring, when we let it ring from every village and hamlet, from every state and city, we will be able to speed up that day when all of God's children—black men and white men, Jews and Gentiles, Catholics and Protestants—will be able to join hands and to sing in the words of the old Negro spiritual, "Free at last, free at last; thank God Almighty, we are free at last."

—FROM "I HAVE A DREAM," MARTIN LUTHER KING, JR

During the Youth Breakfast at the 1999 National Conference of the 100 Black Men of America, Inc. (held in Detroit), Ceaser Shelly, a high school student from New Orleans, addressed the 2,500 participants with these words: "We are the second generation of the children of the civil rights barrier breakers. Invest in us, and we won't disappoint you."

These words have been my inspiration as I have tried to capture the essence and the miracles of mentoring in the pages of this book. My passion for working with young people—and that of my brothers in the 100—is rooted in the experience of growing up in a segregated America and beating the odds with the help of people who loved us, believed in us, pulled us up, pushed us further, and taught us, in the words of movie executive Suzanne De Passe, "to take 'no' as a vitamin."

Many of my generation have succeeded. But that success belongs to our whole community—to the people who made sacrifices to ensure our future and to those who have stood with us, and by us, as we struggled to achieve our goals. Success, as we say in the 100, is not a destination, it is a journey. And the purpose of our journey must be to create a legacy of hope for all God's children.

"We have a wonderful history behind us," writes Carter G. Woodson. "It reads like the history of a people in a heroic age . . . We are going back to that beautiful history and it is going to inspire us to greater achievements." It is, indeed, time for greater achievements. We are no longer just lobbying the system, we have become part of the system and that makes our responsibility so much greater, for when the system fails, it is we who fail.

But we cannot accomplish our goals without recognizing that there is no such thing as partial equality. We must understand and never repeat the slave mentality of the past. We must remember that our minds as well as our bodies are free to do what we need to do, what is in our best interest to do, to move ourselves forward ever further.

We cannot be divisive. We must put our prejudices, biases, and jealousies aside and learn to judge people the way Dr. King did—by their character, not by their gender, color, or faith.

Today, the challenges that face our young people are different and yet the same. Though our children live in an integrated society, they are still in need of a community of support, a "village" that will provide the seeds with which to nurture and raise them. Mentoring, whether it's done on a one-to-one basis, in a group, or with support from community organizations and corporations, is the new experience we must give our young people.

"My grandfather, who was the fire chief of Jackson, Mississippi, taught me that the color of your skin sometimes determines what people think of you," says Joseph Barnes, a ninth-grader who is mentored by the Jackson chapter of the 100. "But he also taught me that no matter what people say about you—and some will always talk—you have to love and respect yourself. And just as important, you have to love and respect your fellow human beings."

We must honor and value each other. But this alone is not enough. We also have to take responsibility for each other. This is especially true with our children. No one would deny that this country cares for its children, and yet increasingly it is our young people who suffer from the effects of the social changes of the past 50 years.

For example, we are willing to spend billions of dollars each year to build more and more prisons in response to violence, crime, and drugs. But are we willing to stop and spend an hour of our time talking to kids about the environments they live in, their fears, their dreams, their frustrations? There will never be enough prisons to incarcerate the children we have failed—even if our nation's landscape comes to look like the nightmarish one in the movie *Escape from New York*—if we do not begin to reach out to all young people and help them deal with the conflicts, challenges, and contradictions of growing up in this society.

It is said that if you think education is expensive, try ignorance. Tragically, we are paying a heavy price for the ignorance of overlooking our children's needs:

- Our prisons are overcrowded with younger and younger inmates.
- Our hospitals are full of people battling life-threatening illnesses that could have been treated by public health education and adequate preventive medical care.
- Our young people—and increasingly our young women—are becoming infected with the HIV virus in ever greater numbers, because of inadequate preventive education.
- Our communities are threatened by drugs.
- Our neighborhoods are terrorized by violence.
- Our teenage daughters are still becoming pregnant in alarming numbers.
- Our children are joining gangs at younger and younger ages.
- Our America is further and further divided into the haves and have-nots, with poverty spreading like a dark cloud over the land.
- Our public institutions seem less and less willing and able to address these problems, while our trust in the system diminishes day by day.

This is the social climate in which we are raising our children. And many of our youths are losing hope for the future. Just look at the sorrowful messages of the school shootings in recent years in Oregon, Colorado, and Georgia. Whatever the complex causes and explanations, whatever comfort we may seek in psychological profiles and media bashing, the basic truth is that in each of these cases young people used guns to proclaim their despair and their profound pessimism about life.

"As children we are all wounded in some way and to some degree by the wild world we encounter," writes Shelby Steele in *The Content of Our Character*. "From these wounds a disbelieving *anti-self* is born . . . that embraces the world's negative view of us. . . . This *anti-self* can only be contained by the strength of the *believing self*, and this is where one's early environment becomes crucial. If the childhood environment is stable and positive, the family whole and loving, the schools good, the community safe, then the *believing self* will be reinforced and made strong. If the family is shattered, the schools indifferent, the neighborhood a mine field of dangers, the *anti-self* will find evidence everywhere with which to deflate the *believing self*."

We cannot protect our children from the wounds of childhood. Disillusionment, pain, and loss—and the self-doubt that comes with them—are a natural part of the human experience. What we *can* and *must* do is help young people build up their immunity to self-doubt. We have to help them develop strength and resilience of character—to become leaders in their own lives.

Raising Real Leaders

I have five children, and one thing I have learned and continue to learn as a parent and mentor is that you cannot live through the children in your life. You must not try to make young people into who you want them to be, but give them the love, support, and encouragement to be the people they want to be. As the poet Kahlil Gibran wrote: "Your children are not your children, they are the sons and daughters of life's longing for itself." You must show them how to take ownership of their lives and how to develop the leadership skills they will need to reach their full potential.

"Courage may be the most important of all virtues," says Maya Angelou, "because without it one cannot practice any other virtue with consistency." And courage is what it takes to love with a love that nurtures and inspires. You have to be brave enough to invest your hope in children without limiting their own expectations and dreams. Most important, you have to be brave enough to be real, present, and responsive.

Randy Walker, the mentoring chair of the 100 Black Men of Metropolitan Detroit, told me this story: "One of the hardest times of my life came a few years ago when my mother died. I was just devastated by the loss. I remember it like it was yesterday. I was sitting on the couch at home crying with my wife. I heard the boys coming back from school and quickly started to try to get myself together. 'Randy,' my wife said, 'you've got to let them see you crying. You just lost your mother; they have to know that you have feelings, that you are not made of cement.'

"I knew she was right, but the instinct to hide, to present myself as invulnerable to the kids was so strong. I said, 'I can't. I just can't.' 'You must,' she insisted. 'Who else is going to show them how a man deals with his feelings? You've got to do it for them, and for yourself.'

"I have to tell you, once I got past the initial fear, it was the most cleansing experience to be able to be fully myself with my kids, to talk to them about how I felt, to have them comfort me. And I could see the effect it was having on them. It was like they were growing right in front of my eyes."

The term "empowerment" is used so frequently it has begun to lose its true meaning. But real empowerment has only one definition: Helping people gain the information, confidence, and skills necessary to wield power in their own lives—to set and maintain their own course. "A man does what he must in spite of obstacles, dangers, and pressures," said the late John F. Kennedy, "and that is the basis of all human morality." And such morality is the foundation of real leadership—leadership that allows us to pursue fulfilling and productive lives and that translates into personal missions that hold the common good as the greatest good. When you do the right thing for the right reason, your destiny will always be success.

I define the qualities of real leaders as follows:

- Real leaders stand tall during times of challenge and turn the challenges into opportunities.
- Real leaders understand that the job ultimately must get done, even if, as it most often happens, they have to do it themselves.
- Real leaders do not worry about where the necessary resources are going to come from; they devise a plan for securing them.

- Real leaders do not sit around and ask "Why?" out of fear of the unknown or in an effort to stall; they ask "Why not?" and get the job done.
- Real leaders would rather make mistakes while trying, than ensure failure by doing nothing.
- Real leaders give out before they give up.
- Real leaders keep their calm even when others around them are losing control.
- Real leaders understand that falling down is sometimes part of the journey of standing up.
- Real leaders stand up for what is right even when it is expedient to go along to get along.
- Real leaders understand that the road can often be very demanding, lonely, and frustrating but are willing to accept the responsibility nonetheless.
- Real leaders prepare others to follow and pass the baton to the new generation when the time is right.
- Real leaders know when it is time to move on, even if the best days are yet to come.
- Real leaders recognize the work and contributions of other people.
- Real leaders are always there to turn the lights on in the morning and turn them off at night.

It is our job to help young people develop the necessary qualities so they can thrive and flourish, so they can take their rightful place as the leaders of tomorrow. And mentoring is the most effective way to accomplish this. By meeting our responsibility to young people, we model for them the qualities of leadership.

"My school was adopted by the One Hundred in my freshman year," says Nicole Smith, a 17-year-old graduate of Theodore Roosevelt Bronx High School who is going on to Hampton College. "Rudy Coombs became my mentor, and he will continue to mentor me for the next four years.

"I've learned so much from Rudy. My mother is the most important person in my life, but to see an educated black man help others was really inspiring. I know that as an educated black woman I am going to follow in his footsteps and reach out to people as well. I am especially interested in working with kids—in psychology, social work, or education. Any way I can.

"I can't wait to start college, but I also don't want this time to end. At Roosevelt, the principal used to say that I was second in command. I was involved in everything. I just loved all the activities, all the opportunities. Having a mentor gave me the confidence of knowing that I always had a back-up and was never really alone."

Mentors expand young people's minds, so they can be whatever is within them to be. One child at a time, we help create hope, aspirations, plans, futures. "We are somebodies," proclaims Candace Arthur, a mentee from our Long Island chapter who wants to be a Supreme Court Justice. "This is our era and our time. If we yearn for it, we can achieve it." That kind of confidence and faith is a precious legacy, indeed.

None of us have become successful by ourselves alone; everyone has been helped along the way. Mentors have existed long before the word was coined. As we progress from generation to generation, the system of mentoring has become more formalized, but its intent and effect have remained consistent.

Each of us wants the next generation to achieve more. Because of our commitment and faith, we are now working harder and broadening the circle of inclusion to make sure that future generations have a better life and a better world than we now enjoy. We cannot and must not restrict our effort by zip codes. The crown jewels of our society are located everywhere, and we must provide support and give our time to polish these jewels so we can all admire and enjoy their brilliance and beauty.

Mentoring is a life-affirming cycle that never really ends. As poet Tiaudra Riley so eloquently writes in "The Circle of Faith":

I have faith in you because I trust you.

I trust you because I like you.

I like you because I care for you.

I care for you because I am a part of you.

I am a part of you because I depend on you.

I depend on you because I am honest with you.

I am honest with you because I can talk to you.

I can talk to you because I am for you.

I am for you because I need you.

I need you because I believe in you.

I believe in you because I have faith in you. . . .

Mentoring is an act of faith in the circle of life. It is an act of faith in each other and, even more important, an act of faith in ourselves. As a mentor, you must look inside yourself, find the best parts of your heart, your soul, and your mind and make the choice to share who you are with others—with young people who need your insight, experience, guidance, and love. And in the process of sharing yourself, you'll discover new and uncharted reaches of your personality, your mind, and your spirit.

These are the miracles of mentoring: In reaching out to shape and guide a young life, you invariably transform two lives—your mentee's and your own. And the best part about these miracles is that they are there for anyone with the desire to participate in the circle of faith, the community of caring, and in the nation of the spirit. All you need to do is open your heart and invite a child to share your life.

What You Can Do:

1. Stay true to your vision.
2. Build an inclusive community.
3. Inspire the leaders of tomorrow.

A Helping Hand: Directory of Mentoring Organizations and Programs

If help is given to us, let us accept it . . .

—ARTHUR LEWIS

Following is a sample of some of the excellent mentoring programs and organizations throughout the country. Volunteer opportunities for mentoring young people are also available through local school systems, places of worship, community recreation centers, juvenile justice offices, community shelters, and religious organizations. In addition, a wide variety of community organizations sponsor mentoring programs, including local Rotary Clubs, Kiwanis Clubs, Lions Clubs, Volunteer Centers, Foster Grandparents groups, and 4-H Clubs.

The National Mentoring Partnership advises potential mentors to be persistent: "It may take a while to be matched with a child. Mentoring programs are concerned with the well-being and safety of children and volunteers, and their selection and screening procedures reflect that concern. Don't get discouraged if the program doesn't match your needs. If that happens, ask to be referred to another organization. Becoming a mentor is well worth the effort, so keep trying!"

1. **100 BLACK MEN OF AMERICA:** Mentors African American youth toward improved educational and economic opportunities. 404-688-5100; www.100blackmen.org

2. **THE NATIONAL MENTORING PARTNERSHIP:** Advocates for the expansion of mentoring and is a resource for mentors and mentoring initiatives nationwide. The leading partner on mentoring for **America's Promise**. National office and 19 local partnerships provide information on what to expect from a mentoring relationship; how to run a mentoring program; and what to do to bring mentoring to your workplace, your place of worship, or your community. Lists all mentoring organizations and opportunities by local zip codes. 202-729-4345; www.mentoring.org

3. **AMERICA'S PROMISE—THE ALLIANCE FOR YOUTH:** Recruits mentors on a national basis to help children at risk. Works in partnership with government,

the private sector, the nonprofit world, service groups, and communities of faith. 800-55-YOUTH; www.americaspromise.org

4. THE ANDREW JACKSON YOUNG AMERICAN FUTURES INSTITUTE (AFI): 877-THE-MALE.

5. BIG BROTHERS/BIG SISTERS OF AMERICA: One-to-one mentoring activities in diverse setting and in schools. 215-567-7000; www.bbbsa.org

6. BOYS AND GIRLS CLUB OF AMERICA: Mentors young people by emphasizing educational achievement and career exploration. 800-854-CLUB; www.bgca.org

7. BOY SCOUTS OF AMERICA: Mentors boys from ages 7 to 20. www.scouting.org

8. CAMP FIRE BOYS & GIRLS: Mentors small groups of children in diverse settings. 816-756-9150.

9. CENTER OF THE AFRICAN-AMERICAN MALE (CAAM): 912-430-7894.

10. COMMUNITIES IN SCHOOLS: One-on-one mentoring and tutoring for young people. 800-CIS-4KIDS; www.cisnet.org

11. COMPUTER CLUBHOUSE: Mentors young people from underserved communities in designing computer-based projects. 617-426-2800, ext. 474.

12. CONCERNED BLACK MEN, INC.: 202-371-9229.

13. CONNECT AMERICA: Sponsored by the Points of Light Foundation and its member Volunteer Centers. Will connect you with mentoring and other volunteer opportunities in your community. 1-800-VOLUNTEER; www.pointsoflight.org

14. CREATIVE MENTORING: 302-633-6226; www.creativementoring.org

15. EVERYBODY WINS!: Program for professionals who travel to elementary schools to read to students during lunch hours. 212-965-2281; 202-624-3957; www.erols.com/ebodywin

16. GIRLS, INC.: Mentors girls, particularly those in underserved areas. 212-509-2000; www.girlsinc.org

17. GIRL SCOUTS OF THE USA: Works with girls from the ages of 5 to 17. 212-852-8000; www.girlscouts.org

18. GROUNDHOG JOB SHADOW DAY: Employees bring a young person to work on Groundhog Day, or more often. 703-535-3874; www.jobshadow.org

19. HARLEM RBI: Mentors young people throughout New York City. 212-722-1608.

20. HEWLETT-PACKARD INTERNATIONAL TELEMENTORING: Connects mentors and young people on-line. www.telementor.org/hp/

21. HOSTS CORP. (HELP ONE STUDENT TO SUCCEED): Tutors students in writing, math, and language. 800-833-4678.

22. "I HAVE A DREAM" FOUNDATION: Mentors students in public schools. Upon graduating from the program, each child receives tuition assistance. 888-216-2232; www.ihad.org

23. JACK AND JILL OF AMERICA, INC.: 407-248-8523; www.jack-and-jill.org

24. JUNIOR ACHIEVEMENT: Mentors in the classroom and shows young people how free enterprise works. www.ja.org

25. KAPOW (KIDS AND THE POWER OF WORK): Mentors elementary school children and introduces them to the world of work. 212-840-1801; www.kapow.com

26. LEARNING FOR LIFE: Mentors in

community-based career education programs for young men and women ages 14 to 20. www.learning-for-life.org

27. THE LINKS INCORPORATED: Sponsors links to Success Mentoring Program. 202-842-8686; www.links.org

28. MENTORING USA: One-on-one mentoring with children in schools and community centers. 212-253-1194; www.mentoringUSA.org

29. NATIONAL ASSOCIATION FOR PARTNERS IN EDUCATION: Mentors in school-based programs. 703-836-4880; www.napehq.org

30. NATIONAL BLACK CHILD DEVELOPMENT INSTITUTE: Mentors middle-school youths. 800-556-2234; www.nbcdi.org

31. NATIONAL FOUNDATION FOR TEACHING ENTREPRENEURSHIP (NFTE): Mentors young people in starting their own businesses. 212-232-3333.

32. NYC MENTORING PROGRAM OF THE NEW YORK CITY BOARD OF EDUCATION: Volunteers from business, government, and other associations mentor students of all ages. 718-935-4520.

33. THE SALVATION ARMY: 703-684-3478; www.salvationarmyusa.org

34. SAVE THE CHILDREN: 800-243-5075; www.savethechildren.org

35. TECH CORPS.: Information technology professionals volunteer in schools to mentor young people in developing and implementing technology plans. 781-687-1100; www.ustc.org

36. THE VILLAGE FOUNDATION: 703-548-3200; www.VillageFoundation.org

37. VOLUNTEERS OF AMERICA: Mentors young people across the United States. 800-899-0089; www.voa.org

38. **YMCA OF THE USA:** Offers wide range of mentoring opportunities. 888-333-YMCA; www.ymca.net

39. **YOUTHFRIENDS:** Mentors young people in schools. 816-842-7082; www.youthfriends.org

40. **YOUTH VENTURE:** Mentors young people as they design and start their own community-minded organizations. 703-527-8300, ext. 223; www.youthventure.org

41. **YWCA OF THE USA:** Mentors girls and young women. 888-675-7351; www.ywca.org

The following mentoring organizations are members of **The National African-American Male Collaboration**, Chicago, IL: 312-906-8600:

1. **ALPHA PHI ALPHA FRATERNITY, INC.**, Baltimore, MD: 410-554-0040, ext. 119.

2. **AL WOOTEN JR. HERITAGE CENTER**, Los Angeles, CA: 323-756-7203; awwoten@earthlink.net

3. **ATHLETES AGAINST DRUGS**, Chicago, IL: 312-321-3400; aad@enteract.com

4. **BOSTON HEALTHCREW**, Boston, MA: 617-534-5264; jrich@bu.edu

5. **BOYS' CLUB OF HARLEM**, New York, NY: 212-289-1815; bch@mindspring.com

6. **BOYS TO MEN**, Chicago, IL: 312-269-5951; nshaw@ulc.edu

7. **THE CLUB (ACTION FOR BOSTON COMMUNITY DEVELOPMENT)**, Boston, MA: 617-357-5000, ext. 7512; hillard@bostonabcd.org

8. DUKE ELLINGTON SCHOOL OF THE ARTS, Washington, DC: 202-333-2671.

9. EAST END NEIGHBORHOOD HOUSE, Cleveland, OH: 216-791-0378; nropi@aol.com

10. ERVIN'S ALL-AMERICAN YOUTH CLUB, Clearwater, FL: 727-443-2061; www.ujoma@gte.net

11. FEDERATION OF SOUTHERN COOPERATIVES/LAF, East Point, GA: 404-765-0991; fas@mindspring.com

12. MAD DAD, INC., Omaha, NE: 402-451-3500; www.maddasnational@infinity.com

13. THE MILTON S. EISENHOWER FOUNDATION, Washington, DC: 202-429-0440; www.lynncurtis@msn.com

14. MOREHOUSE ALUMNI ASSOCIATION, Cambridge, MA: 617-253-3991; jswilson@mit.edu

15. NATIONAL CENTER FOR YOUTH ENTREPRENEURSHIP, Washington, DC: 202-293-1800.

16. NATIONAL FOUNDATION FOR TEACHING ENTREPRENEURSHIP, New York, NY: 212-232-3333, ext. 313.

17. NATIONAL INSTITUTE OF RESPONSIBLE FATHERHOOD AND FAMILY REVITALIZATION, Washington, DC: 202-293-4420.

18. THE NATIONAL TRUST FOR THE DEVELOPMENT OF AFRICAN-AMERICAN MEN, Riverdale, MD: 301-887-0100; mendezir@msn.com

19. NATIONAL URBAN COALITION, Washington, DC: 202-986-1460, ext. 13; trablanshorters@sprintmail.com

20. NO DOPE EXPRESS FOUNDATION, Chicago, IL: 773-568-5600.

21. **OLB/FREEDOM FOR YOUTH**, Helena, AR: 870-572-0656.

22. **OMEGA BOYS CLUB**, San Francisco, CA: 415-826-8664; obc@street-soldiers.org

23. **OPPORTUNITIES INDUSTRIALIZATION CENTERS OF AMERICA**, Philadelphia, PA: 215-236-4500; cbe12@aol.com

24. **OUR FAMILY TABLE FOUNDATION**, Atlanta, GA: 404-765-0084; oftf@mindspring.com

25. **PATHWAYS COMMUNITY DEVELOPMENT CORPORATION**, Dermott, AR; 870-538-5235; pathways@vx4500.uapb.edu

26. **PEOPLES CONGREGATIONAL UNITED CHURCH OF CHRIST**, Washington, DC: 202-829-5511.

27. **PINEY WOODS COUNTRY LIFE SCHOOL**, Piney Woods, MS: 601-845-2214; www.pwsschool@aol.com

28. **PROJECT KEEP HOPE ALIVE**, Commerce, TX: 903-886-5030; anthony-harris@tamucommerce.edu

29. **PROJECT 2000 INCORPORATED**, Washington, DC: 202-543-2309; p2000@erols.com

30. **UNIVERSITY OF KANSAS CENTER FOR MULTI-LEADERSHIP**, Lawrence, KS: 785-884-3990; ibldr@dole.lsi.ukans.edu

31. **YOUTH LEADERSHIP ACADEMY**, Milwaukee, WI: 414-344-8919; rtgiles@man.com